THE

Coexist CONSPIRACY

**Globalists and Alinskyites
Community-Organizing the World**

Introduction

This book is dedicated to all those willing to take the time to read, think and seek the truth.

Introduction

My name is Gabriel Underwood, and I'm a messenger with a typewriter. My friends call me Gabe. I fancy myself a political and theological detective of sorts, employed only by my personal desire to find the truth.

It seems to me, the best detectives have had their assistants, helpers, and trusted sidekicks. Sir Arthur Conan Doyle, creator of *Sherlock Holmes*, provided Sherlock with Dr. Watson, who was told by his detective friend, "You have the grand gift for silence, Watson. It makes you quite invaluable as a companion." Agatha Christie ensured Hercule Poirot had a good friend in sidekick Arthur Hastings, who often reminded Poirot of the simple ethical and confidentiality considerations of conducting criminal investigations, such as not to open up other people's mail or to refrain from eavesdropping.

I have you, the reader, and I'd like you to be my co-investigator. The only requirements of the political and theological investigation trade are the ability to read and think. If you don't have the gift of silence, then shout what you learn from the rooftops. (For the record, I do not open other people's mail, although I do eavesdrop now and then.)

Before you decide whether you are qualified to become my trusted sidekick, you need to know a little about your boss. I've lived and worked in Portland, Maine, my whole life, except for a short government-sponsored vacation. I was one of the last men drafted into the army from Maine in 1972. When I returned to Portland in 1975, I went right back to my job on the loading dock. I continued to live on Peaks Island and went to Portland Bible College, obtaining a theological degree, but I never sought to be ordained.

Now retired from the docks after a lifetime of heavy lifting, I spend most of my time reading, writing, and walking around the island with my walking stick and my dog friend named Patton. Abigail and I occasionally take the short ferry trip to the mainland to enjoy shopping and hanging around the Portland Public Library. We often stop for lunch at Three Dollar Dewey's before the ferry ride home. I enjoy a simple retired Mainer's life.

If the boring simplicity of my life hasn't made you shut the book already, then please continue and let me and demonstrate how we will approach this investigation together. A political and theological investigation is an applied science, as well as an art. It involves the study of facts, used to identify, locate, and prove the guilt or innocence of a political and/or theological fraudster. The facts requiring study can only be found after extensive data collection efforts, and the information can only be understood after extensive political and theological forensic analysis. Each case study covered represents a part of the whole. Remember, the only tools needed to continue are the ability to read and think.

The Coexist Conspiracy is NOT JUST a delusional dream spreading the Earth, although it is that and a lot more. The supreme scam is being thrust on the world's inhabitants by the global elites in an effort to convince us to eliminate war, violence, hatred, racism, sexism, homophobia, Islamophobia, and have a fair distribution of the world's wealth and resources. We must pursue a new, improved, supersized one-world order; although I suspect harnessing the wealth and people of the world has a deeply hidden purpose.

This writer takes literary license documenting this investigation, and I freely use colloquial terms such as *scam*, *scheme*, *duplicity*, *caper*, *racket*, and *skullduggery* interchangeably with the words *fraud* and *conspiracy*. Please don't misunderstand; *fraud* and *conspiracy* are perfectly good words. They're legalese for wrongful criminal deception intended to result in financial and personal gain. This author prefers to utilize the entire thesaurus of descriptive terms to describe legal fraud and conspiracy to accurately express my personal outrage at this great deception and trickery playing out in the world today. Join me, and together we'll investigate *The Coexist Conspiracy*.

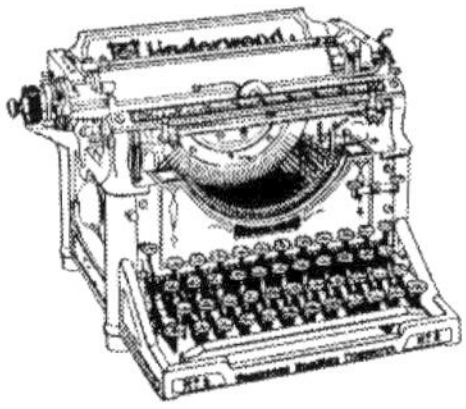

Chapter One
The Case of the Delusional Dreamer

A dream you dream alone is only a dream.
A dream you dream together is reality.
– John Lennon, 1971 –

Our son was home visiting, and for old time's sake, we were enjoying the day roaming around our hometown of Portland, Maine. We decided to have lunch at our favorite pub, Three Dollar Dewey's, on the Fish Pier. As I was enjoying the meal, looking out the front window and listening to the music overhead, I recognized the well-known song from my youth, "Imagine" by John Lennon. I was daydreaming and unaware he was watching me as I enjoyed my beer, ate fried clams, and gently swayed to the music.

He interrupted my Mainer Zen moment with a conversation starter, saying, "Dad, did you know music is part of every culture, past and present?"

I came back from my little trip back to 1972 and said, "How about this one that's playing now, 'Imagine'?" What about 'Imagine'?"

"Sure," he said. "A culture's music is influenced by all aspects of the culture, including social and religious, economic, political, and even the area's climate. For instance," he continued, "as hardy Mainers, you and Mom joyfully sing let it snow, let it snow, don't you?" He explained that the human emotions and ideas that music expresses, the situations it's played in and listened to, and the attitudes music shares, all have a great impact on our culture. He said, "Basically, culture affects our music and our music affects our culture; and that's the long and short of it, Dad."

The Seadogs were playing an away game and it was on the television behind the bar and within our sight. Soon all our talk was of the Seadogs and Boston Red Sox, and how New England has to be the best area of the country, even for sports.

On the way home, I started thinking about what my son and I talked about. I thought, *What does Lennon's song really mean?* On the ferry, I couldn't stop thinking what my son meant about culture affecting music and music affecting culture.

When I arrived home on Peaks Island, I grabbed my headphones, found Lennon's album, filled my pipe with tobacco, relaxed into my recliner, and listened to the words of "Imagine" once again. I meditated on its unity and humanity theme. I thought to myself, *Could the world really coexist without conflict if we had no countries?* All of a sudden, I felt like Sherlock Homes with a magnifying glass looking for a clue, when it came to me . . . it's all a scam. Yes, "Imagine" is some sort of racket. So I listened to it again, wrote down the lyrics, and read them to myself out loud. I'm encouraging you to read them out loud as well. As you're listening to yourself, listen to hear the meaning of the words you are speaking.

Imagine there's no Heaven, It's easy if you try
No hell below us, Above us only sky
Imagine all the people living for today

Imagine there's no countries, It isn't hard to do
Nothing to kill or die for and no religion too
Imagine all the people living life in peace

You may say I'm a dreamer But I'm not the only one
I hope someday you'll join us, and the world will be as one

Imagine no possessions, I wonder if you can
No need for greed or hunger, a brotherhood of man

You may say I'm a dreamer, but I'm not the only one
I hope someday you'll join us, and the world will be as one

John Lennon

I suspect John Lennon's song "Imagine" may be the best example of music with a gently woven underlying deceptive message of social change. Like a tempter, some songs ask a lot of philosophical questions and some, like "Imagine," provide a lot of veiled answers in response. The answers to the questions being asked are found blowing in the winds of fundamental transformation and change for America and the world. "Imagine" is now accepted as the universal song of peace and unity. In fact, President Carter once said, "In many countries around the world—my wife and I have visited about 125 countries—you hear John Lennon's song 'Imagine' used almost equally with national anthems."[i]

President Carter is correct. In fact, it is now the well-established anthem of the progressive liberal left in America, and it is asking us to embrace the anarchy they facilitate, and eventual total government control. I imagine the world had been whispering sweet words of tempting coexistence in John's ears for many years for him to have written the words, "Imagine there's no countries." Then leaning in a little closer, the way the world's scammers do, with another gentle whisper sounding more like a hiss, "It isn't hard to do / nothing to kill or die for / and no religion, too."

It all sounds so familiar, doesn't it? "No borders! No walls! Sanctuary for all!" Lennon sings, "Nothing to live or die for and no religion too." What messages are Lennon and the world really trying to convey? Does he mean that everything I've lived for, fought for, and cared about my whole life—God, family, country, and the Boston Red Sox—are all meaningless?

From my view, "Imagine" is as anti-establishment, anti-American, and anti-God as a message can get. It blows me away that freedom-loving Americans sing it with such enthusiasm. We hold candles and sing about an imagined manmade, safe, comfortable, future utopian coexistence despite all the historical, archeological, and scientific evidence proving the exact opposite. We are unable to maintain peace in our own homes . . . how can we keep peace in the world? Just plain people are often lying, cheating frauds too. And what of the rest of us who are watching this deception and do nothing? Are we all just as guilty?

I'll never forget hearing the painful cries of Rodney King as he was being violently beaten by LAPD officers during his arrest, "Can't we all just get along?"[ii] It was the worst beating at the end of a police baton I've ever seen. The video clearly showed the late Mr. King being beaten repeatedly, and the incident was covered by the news media worldwide. The 1992 LA riots were started over longstanding social issues and lasted six days. The violence ended only after the National Guard re-established peace with overwhelming force, but not before 63 people were killed and 2,373 were injured.

Sorry, Rodney. Sorry, John. The truth is, we will never get along, and the evidence of my belief lies in the simple review of human history and science. The evidence I speak of is easily observable in the socialist construct of comforting lies and fake news being jammed down our throats by a deep-state–controlled media. This essay has been written to reveal the truth as this writer sees it. No fake news here.

During the 2018 World Olympics opening event, viewers heard a performance of John Lennon's classic song "Imagine" performed by a South Korean rock and roll band. The performance of Lennon's song was consistent with the Olympics' "Peace in Motion" theme and emphasized peace, world harmony, and idealism.

Before the Korean musicians delivered the rendition, International Olympic Committee (IOC) president Thomas Bach provided remarks that alluded to the theme. He stated,[iii] "Dear athletes, now, it's your turn! This will be the competition of your life. Over the next days, the world will be looking to you for inspiration. You will inspire us all to live together in peace and harmony despite all our differences. You will inspire us by competing for the highest honor in the Olympic spirit of excellence, respect and fair play."

Since then, Lennon's "Imagine" has become the most successful single of his solo career. The song has been covered by artists in every musical genre, including the meat-dress–wearing Lady Gaga, Stevie Wonder, Neil Young—even Liza Minelli performed it—at some of the world's biggest events, including New Year's Eve and concerts for peace, poverty, and hunger. Willie Nelson recently sang "Imagine" to an audience of fans and fellow superstars. No thinking person can deny the impact John Lennon's "Imagine" has had upon the young people of the world.

The inability of mankind to coexist has always been its greatest hurdle. We are not nearly as enlightened or civilized as we imagine ourselves to be. Humanity demonstrates its inability to get along with each other within our families, our friends, and coworkers, every day. How, then, do we expect nation-states to get along? History shows mankind's inability to coexist has been ongoing since the beginning of time. There has never been a time in world history since the establishment of nation-states that has been absent of war.

History, Scripture, and archeology all confirm that civil unrest and war, which is the extreme result of humanity's inability to coexist, began when humans started forming communities and became less tribal and nomadic. They began storing resources, such as food, clothing, and tools, which were all wanted and needed by others. They had to fight off invading tribes to protect their families and land.

As these communities organized, they became better at repelling their enemies who wanted to steal their stuff, rape their women, kill their children, and take their land. Weapons and defense techniques were developed to serve as the tools and methods of warfare. From the building of a simple spear to the development and use of the A-bomb, mankind has skillfully developed almost every imaginable way to kill each other. It is nothing new that the world is full of hate. People and nations continue to seek to destroy each other for power and possessions . . . even today. Can you just "Imagine"?

Mankind has tried every form of government conceivable to the human mind—city kingdoms, monarchy, democracy, socialism, and communism. Man has attempted every way possible to govern himself without greed and corruption.

The world's governments continue fighting each other, stealing each other's land and possessions. In the social construct of the globalist mind is the foundational belief that for war to exist, nations or nation-states must have a sense of independence and detachment from other communities and without this independence, there will be no potential for conflict. Brick by synthetic brick, the world is attempting to build a tower of coexistence on a foundation of manmade bricks of unity and humanity.

As the investigation continues, we will be studying the facts of each case; not the fake news, just the facts. We will attempt to identify, locate, and prove the guilt of any and all political and theological fraudsters during the course of the investigation.

Beware the Delusional Dreamer.

> *"Now I understand what you have to do.*
> *Put your political message across with a little honey."*
>
> — *John Lennon* —

Chapter Two
The Case of the Conniving Con

I'm sick and tired of hearing things from
Up-tight short sided narrow-minded hypocrites
All I want is the truth, just give me some truth.
— John Lennon, 1971 —

The quest to coexist has been championed by globalist elites since the end of World War II. It's a racket to harness people and their wealth on a global scale, with or without their complicit knowledge. This dream is not just the dream of the global elite. It is now being dreamed by the man on the street due to aggressive socialist community-organizing propaganda efforts of the last 75 years. In his best-selling book *The Art of the Con,* author R. Paul Wilson teaches his readers how to think like a hustler to avoid being scammed. He states, "If I know what you want, I can take everything you have."

R. Paul Wilson is referring to scammers like Alves dos Reis, who was born in Lisbon, Portugal, in 1896. When artful Alves was only 28 years old, he printed himself so much counterfeit money that he caused an economic crisis, leading to a nationalist military coup d'état. Even bolder than Alvi's little scamaroo . . . how about Victor Lustig, who in 1925 infamously sold the Eiffel Tower—twice! Victor did his dastardly homework learning how expensive the tower had become to maintain and he came up with a scheme to sell the Eiffel Tower for scrap. Victor found the most gullible scrap metal dealers he could find. Con artist Victor even managed to pad the bill with a sizeable bribe added for good measure, and even ultimately escaped the law.[iv]

How about the old 1990s email scam with someone claiming to be a Nigerian prince saying he desperately needed help smuggling wealth out of his country? All you, the target, needed to do was provide a bank account number or send a foreign processing fee to help the prince out of his jam. He pleads with you and says he would show his immense gratitude with a generous kickback. Millions of dollars' worth of folks fell for this scam, and still do even today! Imagine?

More recently, not so fortunate financier and fraudster Bernie Madoff was caught operating probably the largest Ponzi scheme in world history, and the largest financial fraud ever in the United States to date. Madoff's brother Peter was the senior managing director and chief compliance officer. He went to jail and is serving a 10-year sentence. Bernie was sentenced to 150 years in prison; his son Mark committed suicide by hanging two years after his father's arrest. [v]

Corporate and individual scammers are adjusting the scams frequently to stay ahead of law enforcement. Some common types of scams everyday working folks like you and me are exposed to include mortgage scams artists, debt elimination scams, telephone, and time share scams. These scamming con artists create websites, television and radio commercials, and even companies that mimic legitimate programs and organizations. They are designed to make suckers like you and me believe we are dealing with legitimate organizations. Remember Victor's scrap metal scam?

How about the simple driveway sealer scam? This racket often targets the elderly, and it's one of the most popular scams in America. It's the classic bait and switch scam. A friend of mine I meet with for conversation and a beer at Three Dollar Dewey's once in a while told me the story of how he was recently scammed out of $800. Art is a 98-year-old veteran, and the soldier who reportedly fired the 90 mm gun shooting down the very first German plane on French soil on D-Day. There was a day when Art recognized the enemy and was trained and ready to face him.

Today, this brave and usually discerning elderly man got scammed out of his social security money. His experience with a door-to-door scammer left him so angry with himself for letting his guard down, he initially didn't want to share his story with the police or local press. But over a couple cold beers and some deep-fried Maine clams, he shared his experience with me.

Art said the smiling scammer told him he had extra sealant after finishing a couple other properties and would do his driveway for $200. Art told me he used to seal it himself, but gave up heavy lifting after he turned eighty. He continued to have his driveway sealed every couple of years at twice the cost he was now being quoted, so he took the smiling scammer up on his offer. Art said he spoke up and told them they weren't covering some cracks, so the smiling scammer feigned getting more sealant.

Once the project was done, the scammer asked for the final price, and to Art's surprise, that $200 job was much more expensive. Eight hundred dollars more expensive! "I was really taken, but I've learned my lesson. I'm not going to let nobody scam me no more." We finished our fried clams and beer over conversation of grandchildren and in his case, great-great-grandchildren.

The Coexist Conspiracy is fraudulently attempting to community-organize the world brick by scheming, manmade brick. The spiritual and cultural war taking place within the open borders of America has rapidly escalated since my youth. Art was a member of The Greatest Generation, as journalist Tom Brokaw in his 1998 book referred to it. Art grew up in Portland, survived the Great Depression in Portland, left Portland to fight in World War II, and returned home to Portland to work and support his family. It's too bad he had to get scammed in Portland.

My generation has been called the generation of free love. I will agree; young people were jumping on the "Peace Train" with

Cat Stevens and hammering out danger with Peter, Paul, and Mary, all while searching for their true inner peace while listening to Bob Dylan's "Blowin' in the Wind." History sets the context for the present, and I fear the desire of the greatest generation to provide their children with more than they had has resulted in the generation of free love spawning the millennial generation of delusional little fishes ripe for the bait, hook, line, and sinker of the global elites to reel them into the new world order.

Many influential historical and contemporary political figures are working this supreme global scam, and old Gabe is naming names in this investigative report. To help highlight their role and function in this skullduggery, I have designated them as the supreme scammer, the super scammer, and soldier scammers. These one-world-government con artists have been manipulating the political and financial events of the world with their global organizing efforts for decades.

This investigation will clearly demonstrate to the reader that our struggle is not against flesh and blood, but against the rulers and powerful world forces of darkness and wickedness in high places; like the world's bad guys identified in this book. These first-rate scammers are educated; they claim personal enlightenment, and they are very wealthy. In fact, they are so rich and puffed-up with themselves and their role in this world, they often believe they are their own gods. These facilitators of folly are mostly from Europe and America, and have rejected the natural stone provided by creation and instead opt for new and improved synthetic stone formed with an aggregate mix of their own inflated unity and humanity.

With deep-state government corruption, looming national debt, an opioid crisis killing tens of thousands yearly, superbugs already killing millions, America's involvement in continuous war, and the breakdown of the traditional family, sometimes I feel like-my head is going to explode with man's inhumanity to man. The deceit and deception woven through the social construct of the globalist mind is astounding to witness.

Have you ever asked yourself, "What is this world coming to?" The answer is, a global scam to community-organize the world into a new world order. Beware the Conniving Con

Chapter Three
The Case of the Synthetic Stone

I planned each charted course
Each careful step along the byway
And more, much more than this
I did it my way
– Frank Sinatra –

Shakespeare wrote, "The past is prologue."[vi] He knew the past is important in explaining the present, and it is a good indicator of what's to come in the future. In fact, there is nothing new under the sun. To ensure a thorough political and theological investigation, this detective of deception and deceit continues with an investigative tactic to pursue a historical understanding as it applies to what's going on in the world today.

I soon found my investigation needed to go further back than Frank Sinatra, John Lennon, and the 1970s. I knew this study needed to go deeper and survey the entirety of recorded history and Scripture to find answers. I went to my cold case file of accepted historical and scriptural truth so commonly being ignored today. Immediately, I found evidence during the genesis of history and Scripture telling us of a time long ago when all the people in the world spoke one language. The political and theological evidence found relative to this investigation has been overwhelming, and has been summarized for clarity.

The first attempt to community-organize the world into a one-world order occurred during the genesis of civilization. As the story goes, people migrating from the East found a plain in the land called Shinar, in Babylonia, and settled there. They wanted to build a city and a tower that would stretch to the heavens and demonstrate their unity and humanity. Falling for the supreme scam, they decided to use improved, manmade bricks instead of natural stone. Filled with self-importance, and stone by synthetic stone, mankind has been making a prideful attempt to build a better world in opposition ever since.

34

After the great flood but before Babel, God said to Noah, "Be fruitful and multiply and fill the earth." The Creator of all saw the tower his creations had built honoring their own knowledge, unity, and humanity, and said, "See, they are one people and all have one language. This is but the beginning, and now nothing they plan to do will seem too difficult for them. Come, let us go down and confuse their language, that they may not understand one another."[vii]

For his glory, God stopped the unruly children of Adam from their community-organizing efforts and made them leave the land and scattered them all over the world. He confused their language, and the tower and the city were named Babel, which appropriately means "confusion." You might be asking yourself how this Sunday school story from thousands of years ago fits in with what's going on in the world today. What was the people's crime? Was it really their pride in their unity and humanity?

Let's unpack the story a bit, pull out Sherlock's magnifying glass and examine both the scam and the Creator's following judgment. The first fist-shaking, sky-screaming, self-promoting departure from the Creator's plan came when the people began to build a city and a tower that reached to the heavens to avoid all the work of "replenish the earth."[viii]

I imagine Babel had challenging economic pressures with tight credit and environmental issues, among other factors, as building projects do today. It was the greatest construction project since the beginning of time! I read somewhere it was called the Babel Big Dig! Think about the graft this scam was going to reap from the people. I can see the scammers of the day falsifying billing records, billing for unperformed work, diverting costs—so much corruption can be hidden in time and material, especially cement. They built the tower into the heavens as a way to make a name for themselves. The story doesn't mention the construction fraud and scamming that must have accompanied the Babel project. Much like John Lennon, I can "Imagine" it too.

Imagine for a moment I am the Ghost of Construction Scams Past, and you've joined me as we attend the last preconstruction meeting for the city of Babel. Up to this point, participants in the process have been satisfied, and everybody is in agreement with the original design using natural stone. The previous construction meetings have all gone well, with the usual rabbit trails and sidebar discussions about the big game or everybody's plans for the weekend.

Today, instead of just coffee, the committee is enjoying a table of fresh fruit, meat, cheese, and bread set before them by the project manager, Mr. Abaddon. During the previous preconstruction meetings, conversation centered on the fluff and puff of it all and how wonderful reaching their unity and humanity goal at the project's completion would be.

Mr. Abaddon's tactic to not go outside the expertise of his people was working well. It was a honey of a hoax. He understood that full transparency too early in the preconstruction process could easily result in confusion, fear, and retreat from the entire project. Each meeting, Abaddon sweet-talked the committee, tactfully avoided discussion, and never fully shared the details of the project. The most important detail on how to obtain the needed natural stone and the projected cost of doing so were never discussed.

The Belial Brothers General Contracting Company and Mr. Belial, the owner, and his legion of his subcontractors, are present. Mr. Abaddon, the project manager, is the last attendee to enter the room. He spreads his blueprints out on the table and informs the committee he and his team have decided to use manmade brick instead of natural stone. It is the old bait and switch. Although the thought crosses everyone's mind that Mr. Abaddon might be taking advantage, they all think he is a nice guy and everybody likes him.

Mr. Belial, their boss, is his good friend and golfing buddy. Abaddon informs the group that while stone is a beautiful, natural material, "They are heavy, difficult to handle, and hard to cut. But, a manmade brick, a synthetic stone, if you will . . . is better!" He asserts that manmade brick can be formed into any shape and size, and because it is manmade, it's flexible, making it better than natural stone. Mr. Abaddon adds, "It is a reasonable economic compromise as we work to improve our circumstances for unity and humanity."

Mr. Abaddon is well-spoken, handsome, and a snappy dresser. He does not demand or persecute—he skillfully persuades; or some would say, beguiles. Abaddon knows if you push a negative hard enough, it will push through and become a positive . . . so he pushes. He artfully makes his way seem better by bringing out new, improved, modern methods and materials to construct Babel. Abaddon understands what he needs to do; put the message across with a little honey.

The reality is, my investigation into the Bible has revealed that our Creator's desire for us is we find our comfort and security in him and in his ways, and not find our security in manmade bricks. The sinful nature of man in the city of Babel was just like it was back in the Garden of Eden, and is even today. People listen to the "hisspers" and guidance of the world scammers rather than their Creator, God. They love the sweet-tasting honey of comforting lies as opposed to the plain-tasting truth. Ultimately, people decide for themselves, because the Creator has given us free will.

It is interesting to note, the Bible story tells us the Creator of the entire universe came down to see the city and the tower, which the "children of man" or "the sons of Adam" had built. The Creator viewed this behavior as sinful in the same way as when

Adam rebelled against God and ate of the tree. The sinful nature of Adam goes on through his descendants. It's called inherited guilt and corruption, or original sin. The story continues, saying the Lord *came down* to see the city and the tower.

I think the author of Genesis is mocking the self-promoting tower-building efforts of the unruly children, saying God had to *come down* to see it because it's soooooo little . . . God can't see it from Heaven. Who said God doesn't have a sense of humor? God was poking fun at how little the tower really was in relation to him and his glory. God sees everything, everywhere, and he doesn't need a manmade brick tower. The prideful, manmade brick designed to improve the living conditions of humanity during the Babel days affects every function of mankind today. The red thread of corruption and fraud is woven through every industry and discipline.

The pharmaceutical industry, known as "Big Pharma"; the Food and Drug Administration (FDA); and the medical industry, are primarily responsible for the consequence of antibiotic resistance and the widespread overuse and misuse of antibiotics, resulting in the development of the dreaded superbug.

Compounding the manmade problem is the non-therapeutic use of antibiotics in animals for human consumption to enhance the animal's growth. It is helping to kill humanity instead of healing us. I don't know about you, but I've been grilling and eating these critters for sixty-plus years. Even low amounts of antibiotics can trigger a bacterial stress response and cause hideous mutations. This means that bacteria subjected to low levels of antibiotics can develop resistance traits faster. Unfortunately, in many countries, including the United States, nearly all clinically essential classes of antibiotics are actively used as food additives for cattle, swine, and poultry.[ix]

As I revealed in my book *THE END IS NEAR*, I was severely injured in the army during combat training in August of 1973. I was airlifted to Walter Reed Army Hospital. I had the kind of injury a young soldier doesn't talk about, especially in mixed company. It wasn't heroic. No Purple Heart was awarded, and none was expected. I was struck in the boys with an unpadded pugilist stick, resulting in a torn bladder and other assorted unpleasantries. Surgery was successful, and I was returned to duty with a P1 profile, which is army lingo for "you're in great shape, soldier, and ready to fight once again."

I returned to my duty as a military policeman (MP), and here's the short story: I've had a wonderful life and I'm not complaining. I married Abigail in 1978, and we are blessed with three children; and as of this writing, we have two grandchildren. Our Creator God is good. The only unfortunate result I was left with was frequent urinary tract infections, all requiring treatment with antibiotics, for the rest of my life.

Penicillin was the first of the miracle drugs to be discovered, and it was my go-to drug for years. Before its introduction, there was no effective treatment for infections, such as urinary tract infections, pneumonia, gonorrhea, or rheumatic fever. Hospitals were full of septic people with blood poisoning contracted from a simple cut, scratch, or urinary infection.

Antibiotics are compounds produced by bacteria and fungi capable of killing, or inhibiting, competing microbial species. This historical truth may explain why the ancient Egyptians had the practice of applying a poultice of moldy bread to infected wounds.[x] But it was not until 1928 that penicillin, the first true antibiotic, was discovered.[xi] The discovery and development of antibiotics are two of the greatest advances in therapeutic medicine. Since the discovery of penicillin and the introduction of it during World War II, countless lives have been saved, including mine.

During the 1980s, the world was scammed with the old bait and switch we saw back in Babel. They switched from natural antibiotics to synthetic medications called fluoroquinolones. Again, we chose manmade bricks as opposed to natural stone. For me personally, this was a big change. I was getting older and experiencing more frequent and severe urinary tract infections. I thought, and so did everybody needing them, that the discovery of this new class of medication was wonderful, and it seemed the manmade answer to a lifetime of pain.

Nothing seemed to rid me of these evil bacteria bugs better than this new, improved, synthetic ~~stone~~ medication. The drug industry skillfully convinced physicians, pharmacists, nurses, and everybody taking natural antibiotics that synthetic ~~stones~~ medication works better. Big Pharma has their share of well-spoken, snappy-looking folks skillfully persuading and beguiling as they introduce new, improved medications too.

I hardly missed a day of work on the loading docks in my forty-plus years. Like I said, I've had a great life. However, the curse of the synthetic medication is in its longsuffering. It kills you slowly with its prescribed cure. Many people suffer tremendous long-term side effects, such as peripheral neuropathy and tendinopathy, among many others. Some folks have even lost all function of their legs and are left unable to walk. Others have experienced walking difficulties, retinal detachments, and bladder and bowel incontinence as a result.

I am one of the fortunate ones; I'm still walking. Nevertheless, I remain the Angry Accuser. I'm not angry with the army or the Veterans Administration; they've been good to me. I'm not even angry with the FDA or the drugmakers who knew the severe, long-term side effects of synthetic antibiotics for nearly ten years before the FDA published its warning on August 8, 2013. This investigation has revealed deeper and darker reasons for their failure to communicate this to the public.

The rulers of darkness seated in high places understand the resistance to existing antibiotics and the fact they may soon kill millions of people unless we find new ones to address the exponentially growing resistance. Due to the skullduggery of the drug industry, the development of new antibiotics has been in decline for years due to the cost-versus-profit ratio. Pharmaceutical companies are already making billions, and are only interested in working on the diseases and drugs that make a huge profit. They are more than willing to spend billions helping mankind get an erection, but not one more dime for real infection control. The inexpensive synthetic options are still working for the industry, treating routine infections regardless of the long-term and potentially deadly effects. Yet, without new antibiotics, millions of people are going to continue to die each year.

What about the opioid crisis? Do you know the difference between opiates and opioids? Classically, the term *opiate* refers to natural substances that come from opium. Examples of opiates are morphine and codeine. Opioids are manmade products that work by binding to the same pain receptors as opiates, but do not occur naturally in the world; they are known as synthetic opioids.

The opioid crisis has been declared a public health emergency. According to the Center for Disease Control, forty-two thousand people were killed by this epidemic in 2016, and it's growing every year. This epidemic is now considered to be the deadliest drug overdose crisis in American history, and is now the leading cause of death for Americans under 50.[xii] A deadly scam to be sure.

Almost twenty years after the introduction of synthetic antibiotics, Big Pharma started facing pressure from the medical industry to treat chronic pain more aggressively. Those same well-spoken, snappy-looking folks skillfully persuading and beguiling were at it again, encouraging doctors to treat pain as a "fifth vital sign" as they introduced new, improved, manmade medications.[xiii] Student nurses were taught a patient's pain is as severe as they say it is and to treat it accordingly. Physicians started recommended the long-term use of opioids—such as OxyContin—for chronic pain. At the same time, pharmaceutical companies began marketing these drugs to medical providers as not addictive or harmful. As a result, doctors began prescribing them at greater rates. According to the Centers for Disease Control and Prevention (CDC), by 2015, enough pills were being prescribed to medicate every American around the clock for three straight weeks.[xiv]

These synthetic ~~stones~~ opioids are highly addictive, and the longer you're on them, the greater the risk of addiction. Opioids are increasingly misused. Sharing these drugs taken from family and friends has become a growing problem. Doctors have also come under fire for overprescribing, either by writing a prescription when it wasn't necessary or by writing prescriptions that covered a weeks-long supply when a few pills would be enough.

Today, the prescription opioids are harder to get legally, mostly because of recent efforts to crack down on excessive prescribing and enhanced law enforcement efforts. Looking for alternatives or cheaper options, some turn to heroin or black market fentanyl. Fentanyl has its own dark and ugly story. It's a powerful anesthetic, up to 50 times more potent than heroin and 50 to 100 times more potent than morphine. Fentanyl is often prescribed to relieve severe chronic pain, including the pain of dying.

My friend Steve, who works the night shift at Portland General, tells me he caught a fentanyl-using coworker stealing the topical patches off dead bodies and chewing them to get his high. Can you imagine? Today, fentanyl is manufactured illicitly and sold on the streets. Much of it is coming with the drug-dealing cartels that freely move back and forth via the open Mexican border.[xv] From 2010 to 2015, annual overdose deaths involving opioids increased nearly 57 percent, largely due to the spike in use of fentanyl and other synthetic opioids.

Even our diet and nutrition fall victim to the supreme scammer and his evil ways. When you were a kid, your mother told you to eat your vegetables because she knew natural foods promoted good health. She also told you, "You are what you eat." Sadly, many of the foods that are manufactured and processed today are actually leading to poor health; diabetes, high blood pressure, heart disease, and even cancer.

I've offered you the evidence, so here's the scam; humanity wasn't meant to die from heart disease, heart attacks, strokes, diabetes, or from cancer of the lungs, breast, prostate, and colon. Prior to the late eighteen hundreds or so, mankind's primary objective each day was to eat enough to be able to work, and to not starve. Obese people were rare.

It was the 1950s; we had beloved General Dwight D. Eisenhower as our president and the postwar economy was booming. Work was plentiful and wages were up. People could afford diets rich in animal products, and the food industry began producing highly processed foods crammed with calories and emptied of nutrition; fast-food chains emerged. We weren't satisfied with the size—how terrible things were!—so everything had to be supersized. McDonald's even still offers a Value

Meal consisting of a Big Mac, large fries, and a Coke with over 1,100 calories and 56 grams of fat; and only God knows how many unhealthy additives.

The social construct of deceit and deception is visibly woven through our manmade, synthetic world. You don't need to be a dietician to understand that natural is better than synthetic, especially when it comes to food. Many diseases can be avoided if we stick to the wholesome food our Creator God has provided for us to eat. But, don't let your guard down; the supreme scammer has many manmade processed foods, clearly unhealthy synthetic options, disguised as healthy foods. Beware the Synthetic Stone.

Chapter Four
The Case of the Organizing Scheme

Telling me the things you're gonna do for me . . . takin' it to the streets,
Takin' it to the streets, takin' it to the streets
— Doobie Brothers, 1975 —

Fast-forward from Babel to Portland, Maine, where I grew

up on Peaks Island, taking the ferry to school each day. It was

1971, and I was in my last year of high school. I was preparing to

follow my older brother into the army and then to Vietnam.

President Richard Millhouse Nixon was our president, and war

against the spread of Communism was raging in Vietnam.

At the same time, a socialist community organizer named

Saul Alinsky was writing his last essay. It was a world-changing

instruction manual of subversive tactics called *Rules for Radicals*.

While forty-eight thousand Americans were laying down their lives

for their country, good old Saul and his not a rock and roll band of Alinskyite community organizers were taking it to the streets, equipping young America with future generations of radical socialists, anarchists, and wannabe Communists. Saul may not have been musically inclined, but he sang the song of the radical left to my generation like nobody before him. So, who is Saul Alinsky? Who are the Alinskyites?

My investigation reveals Saul David Alinsky was born January 30, 1909, in Chicago, Illinois, and died in Carmel, California, in 1972. He is considered the leading American social organizer who stimulated the creation of numerous activist citizen and community groups. After college, Alinsky began his organizing quest in a working-class area of Chicago; the result was the forming of the Back of the Yards Council, which became a prototype for a generation of community organizations.

In 1940, Alinsky founded the International Area Foundation and trained hundreds of young people to become community organizers with his Train the Radical Trainer programs.[xvi]

In his hometown of Chicago, Alinsky helped create the Woodlawn Organization, which successfully organized black inner-city residents to fight the power of the University of Chicago. Saul Alinsky, the community organizer who had organized the Back of the Yards group, was there to lead their work. Saul and the Industrial Areas Foundation organizers succeeded in procuring funding from the Catholic Church, a Presbyterian church, and the Schwarzhaupt Foundation, to begin an organizing campaign in Woodlawn.[xvii]

Super Scammer Saul wrote the first of his three books, *Reveille for Radicals* (1946), while serving a term in jail; his other books were *Rules for Radicals* (1971) and a biography of John L. Lewis (1949). He continued his organizing activities up to the time of his death.[xviii]

Today, we are more familiar with the current adherents to Alinsky's ideology than we are with Saul himself. Soldier

Scammer Hillary Clinton, and of course my favorite radical scammer in chief, President Barack Hussein Obama, are two that immediately come to mind. Although, we now have a couple of newcomer scammers joining the Alinskyite Band in Sen. Elizabeth Warren (D) from Massachusetts, Rep. Alexandria Ocasio-Cortez (D) from New York, and Rashida Tliab (D) from Michigan, who took her oath of office on the Qur'an.

For historical purposes, I'll focus this portion of the essay on veteran Alinskyites such as Bill, Hill, and Barry O. These scamming socialists have exploited the weaknesses inherent in our American system and way of life. *Rules for Radicals* #6 states, "*A good tactic is one your people enjoy.*" I'm pretty sure Mr. Abaddon enjoyed scamming the folks in my imagined story about Babel. Is there anybody on the face of the Earth that doesn't think Bill, Hill, and Barry O don't really enjoy what they're doing? They stay in the public focus and keep doing it without urging and come back to do more. They're doing their thing, and even suggest better scams to pull on the American people and the world.

This terrible trio skillfully scammed and split the American people into two clearly distinct opposing forces, one against the other, over the last two decades. They have opposed any independent, morally strong people, such as American Tea Party members and now the supporters of our current president. This gang of deceiving community organizers has successfully usurped our constitutional rights with social construction, doublethink, groupthink, and lies. Alinskyites engage in large-scale scamming and social engineering projects, creating chaos, with the end goal to reshape the world as they think it should be shaped. They are splitters! They are merely soldiers in the socialist system of the supreme scammer who deceptively whispered sweet words of tempting coexistence in dreamer John Lennon's ears many years ago.

The supreme scammer whispers during his community-organizing gigs and polarizes people by using racial, economic, religious, and political incitements. The supreme scammer, who is also the great accuser, uses the Alinskyite *Rules For Radicals* #13 and will *"Pick the target, freeze it, personalize it, and polarize it."* He uses any tactic that effectively cuts off the support network and isolates the target from any possible sympathy from the masses. He seeks people to hurt because people experience pain deeper and faster than institutions.

However, Rule #13 works very well for institutions as well. The target to freeze, personalize, and polarize is anybody not on board with his deceitful, social justice, rainbow-colored agenda. They are summarily accused of being racist, homophobic, misogynist, and xenophobe. These are the same folks that are chasing people down at restaurants to harass them while they're dining with their families. They organize harassing events in an effort to shut down businesses they disagree with. No conservative or Christian is able to safely publicly speak the truth without fear of harassment and violence. Soldier scammers Bill, Hill, even Barry O, accuse patriots and veterans of being smelly, hillbilly, deplorable, gun-toting, Bible-believing haters. Again, they target to freeze, personalize, and polarize.

The main goal of these scammers is to cause caper-controlled confusion, civil unrest, social instability, and even civil war through subversive and divisive rhetoric. *Rules for Radicals* #2 is "*Never go outside the expertise of your people.*" And Rule #3 is "*Whenever possible, go outside the expertise of the enemy.*" Why? Because these tactics result in confusion, fear, insecurity, anxiety, and uncertainty. The deception is great. Like good socialist scammers, they propose their hope-and-change ideology as the solution.

The supreme scammer, working through Super Scammer Saul and the soldier-scamming Alinskyites, now enjoys a well-established control over the education system in America. They've lowered the standards of education and created a whole dependent class of millennial misfits. The American Teachers Union is made up of largely liberal, Democrat-Progressive socialists who use their political platforms to fill their students' heads with fear, inaccurate history, and a rainbow-LGBTQ agenda. Case in point: Drag Queen Story Hour coming soon to a grade school or public library near you.[xix]

Alinskyite scams are promoting class warfare to the point that hatred and division have caused civil unrest and potential civil war. They use the uninformed, historically ignorant to get the job done. As mentioned, once these America-haters destroy our system of government, they will propose socialism through taxing, redistribution of wealth, and the trumping of your individual, God-given rights as the method to bring about "equality."

Alinskyites appeal to people who want to change the world from what it is to what they believe it should be. Powerful and influential people in high places, like soldier scammers Bill, Hill, and Barry O, have totally bought into the Alinsky ideology and the great deception. In fact, Hillary interviewed Saul and wrote her undergraduate thesis at Wellesley College about Super Scammer Saul and his work. She thought Saul was a super scammer and brought her friend and mentor to Wellesley College in Massachusetts in 1969 to deliver a speech. Clinton stated in her book *Living History*, written in 2003, that she turned down an offer to work with Alinsky after college.

> *I agreed with some of Alinsky's ideas, particularly the value of empowering people to help themselves. But we had a fundamental disagreement. He believed you could change the system only from the outside. I didn't. Later, he offered me the chance to work with him when I graduated from college, and he was disappointed that I decided instead to go to law school. Alinsky said I would be wasting my time, but my decision was an expression of my belief that the system could be changed from within.*[xx]

Hillary believed the system could be changed from within. She supported her husband, Bill, to get elected president; was First

Lady; Senator from New York; and eventually Secretary of State under President Barack Hussein Obama. You can't get more "within" than she was. Some voters from New York still call her a carpetbagger for the New York gig. It certainly worked out for her Clinton Foundation. The Alinskyites are now on the inside of the American government and are the so-called deep state, with a sole mission to corrupt and tear down America from the inside as useful idiots tear it down from the perimeter so they can rescue us, bringing in a one-world order.

Former President Barack Hussein Obama, or Barry O, as he was called in Chicago, was pretty well-schooled in community organizing in the Saul Alinsky tradition. It was an experience Obama recalled as the best education he ever had.[xxi] Although, he said the same thing about a Muslim school he attended in Indonesia as a youth.

President Obama was taught how to be a community organizer via the *Rules for Radicals* by disciples of Saul himself. One of Barack's original Chicago mentors was chief Alinskyite Mike Kruglik. He said Obama was the best student he ever had, a "natural…undisputed master of agitation."[xxii] His description reveals how Obama has been capable of undermining America, inspiring young anarchists by disguising his ideology as simply hope and change.

President Obama repeated the Alinsky call for the "world as it should be" every chance he got, especially when out of the country.[xxiii] This great deception became his mantra. He blamed the United States for the world's troubles and promised a future where the planet will heal from American domination. Soldier Scammer Barry O employed Rule #5: *"Ridicule is man's most potent weapon."* He used this skillfully because there is no defense, and it works well as a key pressure point to force the enemy into concessions.

Take a good look at America and the world today as you think about that one. His "world as it should be" exists only in their liberal minds with government-run healthcare, unfettered abortion, and open borders.

In addition, Barry O's Islam-sympathizing, anti-American, gender something or other, weak militarily, conservative-hating ideology has been easily disguised to the afraid, uninformed, or willfully ignorant. Former President Obama continues to encourage our youth and implement his and the Alinsky ideology every chance he gets. Remember what John Lennon said about dreamers? If anything, now that Barack is out of office and back organizing, he is even more motivated to fundamentally transform "the world as it is" into "the world as it should be" . . .a one-world socialist state. In fact, Soldier Scammer Barry O is a Chicago mobster in the same way his teacher Super Scammer Saul identified himself with the Mob. In an interview with *Playboy* magazine in

1972,[xxiv] Saul Alinsky clearly identified with mob tactics.

ALINSKY: *Sometimes it seems to me that the question people should ask is not "Is there life after death?" but "Is there life after birth?" I don't know whether there's anything after this or not. I haven't seen the evidence one way or the other and I don't think anybody else has either. But I do know that man's obsession with the question comes out of his stubborn refusal to face up to his own mortality. Let's say that if there is an afterlife, and I have anything to say about it, I will unreservedly choose to go to hell.*

PLAYBOY: *Why?*

ALINSKY: *Hell would be Heaven for me. All my life I've been with the have-nots. Over here, if you're a have-not, you're short of dough. If you're a have-not in hell, you're short of virtue. Once I get into hell, I'll start organizing the have-nots over there.*

PLAYBOY: *Why them?*

ALINSKY: *They're my kind of people.*

What kind of people are those, Saul? Demon people? When Saul was asked about his religious beliefs, he always said

65

he was Jewish. His parents were strict Orthodox Jews, and socialist Saul was brought up in the tradition. However, during his life, he distanced himself from his Orthodox Jewish background. In *Rules for Radicals*, when praising Moses as a "good organizer," Saul worded it in such a way one could easily see he was really shaking his angry fist and blaming God.[xxv] He was probably screaming at the sky at the same time.

In an interview with George Stephanopoulos on ABC, then Sen. Barack Hussein Obama was asked about his religion and he referred to "my Muslim faith." His good old buddy George corrected him: "You mean your Christian faith."[xxvi] Who makes that kind of mistake? Nice cover, Soldier Scammer George! Now President Barack Hussein Obama may not be a full-fledged, mosque-attending, prayer rug kind of Muslim, but at the very least he is a cultural Muslim sympathizer. I'll never forget the lie he's been selling us for years: "Islam is a religion of peace." That's all part of the Supreme Scam too. Old Gabe here shares the result of his investigation examining how Islam plays into The Coexist Conspiracy a little later on.

The Alinsky management approach to teaching community organizing sparked a bright young Alynskyite who dubbed him the "Machiavelli for the common man."[xxvii] In *Rules for Radicals*, Alinsky's response to those who ask, "Does the end justify the means?" was "The means and end moralists, or non-doers, always wind up on their ends without any means."

I'll never forget President Barack Hussein Obama referring to working-class voters in old industrial towns decimated by job losses. The presidential hopeful said: "They get bitter, they cling to guns or religion or antipathy to people who aren't like them or anti-immigrant sentiment or anti-trade sentiment as a way to explain their frustrations."[xxviii]

Do you recall when President Obama inserted himself into a racially charged local police situation in the beginning of his presidency?

A personal friend of President Obama's, Harvard Professor Henry Louis Gates, was arrested on the front porch of his home in Cambridge, Massachusetts. Upon returning home from a long trip, the absentminded professor found the front door to his home jammed shut. Gates tried to force the door open with the help of his driver. A nearby resident reported their activity as a burglary in progress to the Cambridge Police. Upon arrival at Gates's home, the police found Gates yelling and screaming, and he was arrested by the responding officer for disorderly conduct. The charges against Gates were dropped.

President Obama went on national television and proclaimed the Cambridge Police "acted stupidly."[xxix] Of course, later it was proved they were just doing their jobs and the absentminded professor had just lost his cool in addition to his keys. Initially, racial profiling was all the talk, but charges against the police were later dropped too. President Obama held the well-known "Beer Summit" at the White House to resolve differences. What a lightweight.

President Obama is a tool, and a mere soldier in the socialism community-organizing ranking. I believe he does what the supreme scammer tells him to do. It appears President Obama and the scamming Alinskyites believe Americans are stupid, irrational, and incapable of knowing what is actually best for themselves. What did John Lennon say about political messages and a little bit of honey? Remember the table of delicious treats set before the legions of subcontractors by Mr. Abaddon? People love the comforting lies rather than an unpleasant truth. The supreme scammer counts on it. If you've been asking yourself, who is the supreme scammer? I'll get to his identity a little later. In the meantime, be a watchman looking for evidence and beware the

Organizing Scheme.

Chapter Five
The Case of the Fraudulent Financier

I'll buy you a diamond ring my friend, if it makes you feel alright
I'll get you anything my friend if it makes you feel alright
— Paul McCartney, 1964 —

Investigative review of publicly available data, newspapers, magazines, books, and the internet reveals Sugar Daddy Socialist Uncle George Soros is one of the richest men in the world today. Don't be too impressed. He too is a mere underling playing in the Alinskyite band. He is not the supreme scammer. He is, however, a highly skilled financial facilitator and super scammer. Uncle George is not just a soldier scammer like Saul, Bill, Hill, and Barry O in the community organizing effort; he's a prince doing his king's bidding. His king is the supreme scammer and great deceiver. According to *Forbes* magazine, Prince George's worth is upwards of $20 billion dollars. Uncle George isn't just a rich scammer; he's a sinfully rich scammer.

George isn't just liberal, either; he's sinfully liberal. In fact, there isn't a liberal radical organization he doesn't financially support. In 1984, Uncle George created his now pet program entitled the Open Society Foundations. Sugar Daddy Soros donated more than $8 billion to charities around the world through this organization. Media Research Center reports Soros has "helped foment revolutions, undermined national currencies and funded radicals around the world."[xxx]

Rules for Radicals #8. **"*Keep the pressure on. Never let up.*"** The guidance is to keep trying new things to keep the opposition off balance. As the opposition masters one approach, hit them from the flank with something new. The lies and deception are all under the direction of the supreme scammer, who has been called the god of the air and the god of the world. For now, let's unpack who the fraudulent financier George Soros is and why I refer to him sarcastically as Uncle Sugar Daddy George.

Born to a Jewish family in Budapest in 1930, George Soros survived the Nazi occupation of Hungary, where more than half a million Jews were killed. As a teenager, Soros worked as a courier for a Jewish council set up by German-occupying authorities to ensure the implementation of Nazi orders. Young George collaborated with the Nazis, now saying he is "not sorry for helping in the confiscation of property from the Jews."[xxxi] He stated this in an interview with Steve Kroft of CBS's *60 Minutes* in 1998.

The scamming started early for Uncle George. He defended himself, saying, "There was no sense that I shouldn't be there, because that was–well, actually, in a funny way, it's just like in markets–that if I weren't there–of course, I wasn't doing it, but somebody else would–would–would be taking it away anyhow. And it was the–whether I was there or not, I was only a spectator, the property was being taken away. So the–I had no role in taking away that property. So I had no sense of guilt."

When deportations from Hungary to death camps began to soar during the Holocaust, George hid his Jewish identity to survive. Not long ago, Nazi collaborator Uncle George was convicted of insider trading in France on behalf of his new world order efforts.[xxxii] Poor George; he had to pay a mere $5 million in fines to France and his native Hungary to keep himself out of jail. His cagey foundations have been accused of everything from shielding spies to breaking currency laws, to investing to harm several national currencies. Media Research Center reports George's support for higher education raises all kinds of red flags.[xxxiii] Soros has contributed more than $400 million to colleges and universities, including money to the most prominent institutions in the United States. Uncle George's super scamming and generosity was extended to help create Central European University.[xxxiv] Super Scammer George now uses the university's resources to promote his personal goals of a worldwide "open society."[xxxv]

George shares his heavy coin freely with the youth of the world.

His children of anarchy and liberal organizations promote their

rainbow-LGBTQ, transgender, and gay marriage agendas, as well as

drug legalization, up to and including anti-death penalty strategies.

This scam is to indoctrinate students and teach them to promote

liberal, and in many cases extremist, causes using the Alinskyite

method.

Morton Abramowitz of the Carnegie Endowment for

Peace once said Soros was the "only private citizen who had his

own foreign policy."[xxxvi] That remains true, through his super

scamming conflicts in the United States, where he is a citizen.

Uncle George Soros devoted much of his early foundation

effort to the former Soviet Union and then its successor republics.

The liberal *New Republic* quoted Soros in 1994 as saying, "Just write

that the former Soviet Empire is now called the Soros Empire."[xxxvii]

Soros is "possibly, fantastically, the single most powerful foreign influence in the whole of the former Soviet empire" they added.[xxxviii]

Many governments view Soros as the enemy because of his new world order finance. It is pretty easy to see George Soros's imprint on most major American left-wing organizations. All you have to do is look at their financial forms. Follow the money. Uncle George aids hundreds of left-wing groups in America each year under the auspices of his Open Society Foundations and under the direction of his leadership. In just 10 years, Soros has given more than $550 million to liberal organizations in the United States. Scammer Saul once said, "The judgment of the ethics of means is dependent upon the political position of those sitting in judgment."[xxxix] Like I said before; Sugar Daddy Uncle George is a super scammer, but a mere prince in the coming new world order.

The Coexist Conspiracy and the subsequent attempt to community-organize the entire world by the supreme scammer is to destroy the United States of America as a nation under

God. He has always hated America for boldly proclaiming we are "under God" and "In God We Trust."

The supreme scammer wants to be god and is working to that end. However, America's foundation is formed with manmade brick using cement of lies and deceit mixed with an aggregate of humanity and unity instead of natural stone . . . and it is crumbling. Even in the Church, the foundation is crumbling and being replaced by man's word.

Rules for Radicals #1: *"Power is not only what you have, but what the enemy thinks you have."* Saul knew power is derived from two main sources: people and money. Therefore, in the Alinskyite ideology, the have-nots must build power from flesh and blood. Just the way the supreme scammer historically likes it . . . from flesh, blood, and the souls of men.

Despite our bold proclamation of exceptionalism, which we base on our unique American history, our nation has fallen out of relationship with God much the same way "we the people" do, and for the same reason . . . sin. We once boasted we were a nation "of the people and by the people." Following that line of thought, America was sure to fall out of relationship with God, because it's a nation of people, and we all have a fallen, sinful human nature and end up shaking our fists at our Creator. The creation thinks he's smarter than his Creator. Imagine.

The United States' Great Society effort in the 1960s was a clear foreshadow to the one-world effort to come. This vision of the Democratic progressive liberal left put into practice a series of legislative and policy initiatives and programs all driven from the inside, top-down, under the direction of President Lyndon B. Johnson, a soldier scammer from my yesteryear, with the main goals of ending poverty, reducing crime, abolishing inequality, and improving the environment, thereby facilitating the making of what President Johnson called the Great Society.

Whoa! Sounds familiar, doesn't it? It didn't quite get to the "No borders, no walls, sanctuary for all!" level . . . but socialism was well on its way into the hearts and minds of America. The war on poverty, Medicare and Medicaid, Head Start and education reform, taxpayer money for the arts and humanities; all were part of the Great Society.

In September 1965, President Johnson signed the National Foundation on the Arts and Humanities Act to study the humanities, as well as fund and support cultural organizations such as museums, libraries, public television, public radio, and public archives. It declared "the arts and humanities belong to all the people of the United States" and that culture is a concern of the government, not just private citizens. Double whoa!! George Orwell once said of government, "Power is in tearing human minds to pieces and putting them together again in new shapes of your own choosing."[xl]

Public television, radio, and the Great Society have had great power and influence in reshaping our minds and contributing to putting them together again in shapes of their choosing from 1948 to the present. I wasn't paying too much attention when I put my children down in front of the TV to watch *Sesame Street* back in the 1980s. I do remember one sensitive and highly publicized episode when Mr. Hooper, a character on the show, died, and Big Bird and all the other Muppets had to learn about grief, death, and its irreversibility. It opened up conversation about a truthful reality . . . everybody dies . . . even Mr. Hooper.

Today, watching *Sesame Street* doesn't just open up conversation, it's a walk down the streets in Bizzaro Land. The Sesame Workshop announced its flagship program is featuring its first transgender character for the 2019 season. According to staff writers, "Brunny" will join Elmo, Big Bird, and the rest of the *Sesame Street* characters to discuss important issues of the day. *Sesame Street* boasts it has a long commitment to multiculturalism and diversity. Bethany Millbright, communication director of the Sesame Street Workshop, said, "So as you might imagine, adding a transgender character to our huge cast of diverse Muppets was a no-brainer. We understand that there will be some who don't understand this addition, but Sesame Street has long been a vanguard of children's television and we believe history is on our side."[xli]

PBS also has announced 2019 shows entitled: *Scientists rethink gender identity with new research* and *Doctors working with transgender individuals are discovering more about the relationship between biology and gender.*[xlii] Like I said before, the creation thinks he's smarter than his Creator. Do you think Mr. Abaddon might be on the board and working with PBS, helping them with their long commitment to multiculturalism and diversity for unity and humanity? If he were, I would bet Sugar Daddy George, who has woven his one-world order deceit and deception liberally through the world, is financing the whole globalist gig. Beware the Fraudulent Financier.

Chapter Six
The Case of the Confusion Caper

There's something happening here,
but what it is ain't exactly clear.
— Buffalo Springfield, 1967 —

Conspiratorial controlled confusion is a description of something that looks out of control yet is functioning according to the designed scam. If you're confused and trying to determine what's real and what's fake, they have you right where they want you. The supreme scammer is the author of confusion and deceit, and it is he who is shaking this world like never before. He has infected the organizations and institutions of the world in an effort to control people by keeping them confused and looking to government for answers. *Rules for Radicals #9. "The threat is usually more terrifying than the thing itself."* According to Saul,[xliii] "Imagination and ego can dream up many more consequences than any community activist." Wow, just imagine.

This discerning detective has determined, using his United Imagine-Nation, that the UN, motivated by the experiences of the preceding two world wars, officially recognized the human right of individuals to move across borders for economic, personal, or professional reasons or to seek asylum and refuge guaranteed by the Declaration of Human Rights. The same declaration supported a basic right to self-government, stipulating, "The will of the people shall be the basis of the authority of government,"[xliv] including the fundamental right to control its borders, as well as determining who is to be a citizen resident or an alien.

Alinskyite scamming has now officially entered the big league. Were you aware that all this migration is a case of controlled confusion? Were you aware that behind your back, President Barack Hussein Obama was soldier scamming the first-ever global compact for migration? If you think the Iran deal was troublesome with Obama's vision of a world without nuclear weapons, the centerpiece of his "we are the world" anti-nuclear weapon agenda was to prevent Iran from becoming a nuclear weapons state by giving them billions of American dollars in cash and gold bullion. The Obama team set out to negotiate a deal that would supposedly roll back the nuclear program and set up a verification regimen to ensure compliance. It never happened, as some predicted.

This investigation has uncovered this attempt to community-organize the world and it's real; it's negotiated and it's in practice. It is the world's first community-organized migration agreement developed and put in place by the United Nations. That fact alone scares the Peter Gunn and Phillip Marlowe right out of this amateur gumshoe.

The UN reports we have more than 68 million migrants around the world living outside their country of birth.[xlv] They expect this figure will continue to grow for reasons including population growth, increasing connectivity, trade, rising inequality, demographic imbalances, and of course, they had to include . . . climate change. What our one-world order community organizers fail to mention is the world is being overwhelmed by forced migration. This investigation reveals millions of people are on the move, fleeing their home countries in search of a better life driven by manmade civil wars, oppressive regimes and economics, and the invitation of those pushing a one-world order through Alinskyite tactics and strategies.

George the super scammer tells us . . .

"The collective failure to develop and implement effective policies to handle the increased flow has contributed greatly to human misery and political instability—both in countries people are fleeing and in the countries that host them, willingly or not. Migrants are often forced into lives of idle despair, while host countries fail to reap the proven benefit that greater integration could bring."[xlvi]

In super scammer George's view, governments must play the leading role in addressing this crisis by surrendering their sovereignty and providing adequate physical and social infrastructure for migrants and refugees with the assistance of the United Nations. George and Barry O won't be happy until the day those new, pretty, white UN vehicles are roaming the streets of Europe and America. They too believe America and Europe will "reap the proven benefit that greater integration could bring."[xlvii]

Soldier scammer President Barack Hussein Obama launched his own call to action, asking US companies to play a bigger role in meeting the challenges posed by forced migration. A long list of American private-sector leaders and billionaires are assembling at the United Nations to make concrete commitments to help solve the problem. Google the footnote for the White House's list and you will see long list of large, well-known organizations; and even Google is listed.[xlviii]

Uncle George was so impressed with soldier scammer Barry O and his soldier scammer effort, he earmarked $500 million for investments specifically for the needs of migrants, refugees, and host communities in his honor. George spreads his wealth through startups, established companies, social-impact initiatives, and even businesses founded by migrants and refugees themselves. His main concern is to help migrants and refugees arriving in Europe, but he freely admits he wants to encourage a free flow of migration and help migrants all over the world.

Uncle George digs this forced migration. By supporting it with his time, talent, and financial treasure, he's a real prince in the supreme scammer's efforts. It's his gig. He has dedicated his life to working on global migration and he has dedicated his great wealth to it. The United Nations is in cahoots with the supreme scammer, who is a great deceiver, and they are trying to convince the world that migration will provide a fair distribution of the world's wealth.

No borders, no walls, and sanctuary for all.

The current forced migration is a supreme scam on the world. The United Nations recognizes the human right of individuals to move across borders for economic, personal, or professional reasons or to seek asylum and refuge guaranteed by the UN's 1948 Declaration of Human Rights. The same declaration supports a basic right to self-government, stipulating, "The will of the people shall be the basis of the authority of government," including the fundamental right to control its borders as well as determining who is to be a citizen resident or an alien.

George Orwell defined doublethink as the act of simultaneously accepting two mutually contradictory beliefs as correct.[xlix] He contended that people learn doublethink due to peer pressure and a desire to fit in or gain status within the organization. Groupthink is similar to doublethink in that it is a desire for harmony or conformity and minimizing conflict to reach a consensus decision. No alternative viewpoints are allowed, and critical thinking is strictly forbidden. Groupthinkers and doublethinkers avoid raising controversial issues or alternative solutions. Individual creativity and independent thinkers are verboten.

Saul and his pride-filled ingroup of dysfunctional Alinskyite scammers have been working with soldier scammers on the inside of America for decades. President Lyndon B. Johnson of the Great Society, Bill, Hill, and Barry O, are all endeavoring to create an illusion of invulnerability for their cause. Remember, *Rules for Radicals* #1: *"Power is not only what you have, but what the enemy thinks you have."* Doublethink and groupthink were clearly a factor in this group of scammers due to their obvious lack of cognitive dissonance. If you consider yourself an honest person and tell a lie and feel uncomfortable about it . . . you have likely experienced cognitive dissonance. Guilt.

According to the field of psychology, *cognitive dissonance* is the mental discomfort or psychological stress experienced by a person who simultaneously holds two or more contradictory beliefs, ideas, or values.[1] The lack of cognitive dissonance experience helps explain the lengths our lying politicians and leaders go, as they apparently feel little mental discomfort or psychological stress with contradicting manifestations of their beliefs. They seem to rather embrace the social construct of comforting lies rather than the unpleasant truth.

It's interesting to note Islam has numerous contradicting manifestations in their belief system. It is referred to as *dualism*. For example, President Barack Hussein Obama and Islamic apologists tell us Islam is a religion of peace, but history clearly reveals it's a religion of jihad and death. The delusional thread of coexistence to accept unchecked migration of Muslims who refuse to assimilate and carry 1,400 years of historical baggage has been woven through governments and institutions throughout Europe and the Americas. Soldier scammers and those desiring to community-organize the world into a one-world government have tactically utilized doublethink and groupthink to spread the coexist delusion.

The United Nations Declaration of Human Rights provides the world with contradicting rights. The declaration states that people have the right to migrate and leave their country of birth. It also ensures nation-states retain the right to refuse entry.[li] The controlled confusion of migration is a stealth weapon of war and has been eroding national borders and weakening sovereign governments, including America, since the end of World War II. Forced migration and the conspiratorial document known as the Migration Compact is a worldwide scam of controlled confusion.[lii]

The United Nations and the global elite, with their international business interests, control everything. Many of our own government officials and politicians are deep state soldier scammers in the coexist conspiracy to community-organize the world into a one-world order and they are there to only give you the illusion of choice. There is no real choice in this world. That's why you were not made aware the UN and the global elite already formally agreed to facilitate unfettered global migration, as well as see to the migrants' comfort as much as possible along the way. These global flimflammers make all the big decisions behind our too-busy-working-earning-our-living backs. They own or control everything, including the state governments, judges, and all the big media companies, controlling just about all of the news and even create the fake news they want you to hear.

The United States has debated immigration since the country's founding. The Statue of Liberty has been a symbol for immigrants, and is often invoked as an argument for why we should allow in those who seek safety and opportunity with open arms. Just as an aside, not to frighten you, in fact, it probably doesn't mean anything in the existential sense, but Lady

Liberty adds an intriguing twist to today's debate about refugees. She is a Muslim refugee.[liii] The statue itself was originally intended to represent a female Egyptian peasant as a new Colossus of Rhodes for the Industrial Age. The Supreme Scammer's woven web of deceit and deception is invasive, infective, and is using the United Nations as a conduit for establishing a one-world order. It's kind of ironic, don't you think? This controlled migration has a deeper and even darker purpose, which this investigative writer shall reveal later. In the meantime, beware the Confusion Caper.

Chapter Seven
The Case of the Social Justice Warrior

You say you want a revolution,
Well, you know
We all want to change the world.
— The Beatles —

The definition of social justice varies with the organization

or individual social justice warrior defining it for you. Their

common themes include human rights and economic equal

distribution of wealth and resources. It was first used by the

Roman Catholic Church for describing a virtue necessary for post-

agrarian societies, which are any society whose economy is not

based on producing and maintaining crops and farmland.

A social justice warrior, or soldier scammer, by this writer's

definition, is a street-wise scammer advocating a socially

constructed, uniform, government-controlled distribution of

society's advantages and disadvantages. Social justice is the capacity to organize people to accomplish ends that benefit the whole community. But does the social justice ends justify the means? The Merriam-Webster Dictionary describes social justice a *"social philosophy advocating the removal of inequalities among people."* Dictionary.com defines social justice as "the distribution of the advantages and disadvantages within a society."

Who is going to be in charge of distributing and redistributing these manmade advantages and disadvantages? These definitions suggest the government, who are all smarter than us, or the proposed one-world order, would be manufacturer and distributer of the world's wealth and resources. "No borders! No walls! Sanctuary for all!" Imagine?

Robert Reich served in the administrations of three presidents. He was Secretary of Labor from 1993 to 1997, and a member of President Barack Obama's economic transition advisory board. He is an entrenched one-world order advocate. In his book *The Common Good,* Reich asserts, "The common good constitutes the very essence of any society or nation."[liv] Societies, he says, undergo virtuous cycles that reinforce the common good as well as vicious cycles that undermine it, one of which America has been experiencing for the past five decades. This process can and must be reversed. But first we need to weigh the moral obligations of citizenship and carefully consider how we relate to honor, shame, patriotism, truth, and the meaning of leadership.

Personally, I understand "social justice" in a similar way as Robert Reich understands the term "common good." It's fairly interchangeable. What is the common good? Back in the Babel days, I'd be willing to bet Mr. Abaddon and Mr. Belial were the wisest and strongest people in the community. Project Manager and Architect Abaddon clearly made the pre-construction decisions, such as where the tower would be built, and to use manmade brick instead of natural stone.

In the utopian world-view of the social justice warrior, who is also a soldier scammer, the responsibility for the common good rests with government. This delusional dream is an open door, the camel's nose under the tent, a slippery slope invitation for authority and total government control. The political and theological fraudster, social justice warrior, and soldier scammer find it necessary to create problems in order to maintain victimhood status. This deceptive phenomenon is a confidence scam woven through the movement.

The Original Rainbow Coalition was formed in Chicago in the late 1960s, and it was the alliance between the Chicago Black Panther Party, Puerto Rican Young Lords, and the Poor White Young Patriots Organization. People came together across racial lines to build power, support each other, and fight for their shared interests. Many liken the original Rainbow Coalition to the Populist Party post-Civil War.

After the Civil War and during the late 1800s, farmers were

suffering from crop failures, falling prices, poor marketing, and lack

of credit facilities, giving birth to the Populist Party. It was a

movement by farmers in the South and Midwest against the

Democratic and Republican parties for ignoring their interests and

difficulties. Some saw it as a threat to the postwar establishment,

and it was dismantled after Plessy v. Ferguson 163 U.S. 537 (1896),

which was a landmark decision of the U.S. Supreme Court issued

in 1896. It upheld the constitutionality of racial segregation laws for

public facilities as long as the segregated facilities were equal in

quality—a doctrine that came to be known as "separate but equal."[lv]

Previously, the Civil Rights Act of 1875 had stated that all

races were entitled to equal treatment in public accommodations.

An 1883 Supreme Court decision clarified that the law did not

apply to private persons or corporations. Here we see the

Confusion Caper in full operation. Confusion about the legality of

segregation continued until challenged by Homer Plessy. After the 1896 Plessy v. Ferguson decision, segregation became even more ensconced through a battery of Southern laws and social customs known as "Jim Crow." Separate but equal and Jim Crow remained unchallenged until Brown v. Board of Education in 1954 and the Civil Rights Act of 1964.

Today, Reverend Jesse Jackson has combined the Rainbow Coalition with Operation PUSH. The Rainbow PUSH Coalition (RPC) is a multi-racial, multi-issue, progressive, international membership organization fighting for social change. Their website states they, "work to make the American Dream a reality for all our citizens and advocate for peace and justice around the world." They continue their doublespeak, saying they are dedicated to improving the lives of all people by serving as a voice for the voiceless. The mission, they say, is "to protect, defend, and gain civil rights by leveling the economic and educational playing fields, and to promote peace and justice around the world."[lvi] No borders, no walls, sanctuary for all!

Black Lives Matter describes themselves as a "chapter-based, member-led organization whose mission is to build local power and to intervene in violence inflicted on Black communities by the state and vigilantes."[lvii] They view their role as a collective of liberators who believe in an inclusive and spacious movement, and believe that in order to win and bring as many people with them along the way, they must move beyond the narrow nationalism they contend is all too prevalent in black communities. They further contend, Black Lives Matter must ensure they are building a movement that brings all of them to the front. The movement boldly proclaims they affirm the lives of black, queer, and trans folks, disabled folks, undocumented folks, folks with records, women, and all black lives along the gender spectrum. They believe black lives are being systematically targeted for demise by the current system of government. The movement, they say, is a rallying cry for ALL black lives striving for liberation.

The Black Lives Matter movement, whose stated mission is to affirm "Black folks' contributions to this society, our humanity, and our resilience in the face of deadly oppression,"[lviii] has a flawed ideology of reparatory racial exclusion that is clearly illustrated in Lisa Durden's Fox News interview.

Durden, a professor of media and effective speech at a New Jersey community college, made a televised appearance on *Tucker Carlson Tonight*, where she defended Black Lives Matter's decision to preclude people who do not identify as black from attending a Memorial Day celebration organized by the movement. Carlson began the interview by reading an excerpt from a statement disseminated by the movement regarding the controversy. He read, "Being intentional about being around Black People is an act of resistance. This is an exclusively Black Space so if you do not identify as Black and want to come because you love Black People, please respect the space and do not come."

"I'm confused by that," Tucker said, "because I thought the whole point of Black Lives Matter . . . would be to speak out against singling people out on the basis of their race and punishing them for that, because you can't control what your race is, and yet they seem to be doing that. Explain that to me."

"What I say to that is boo hoo hoo," Durden replied. "You white people are angry because you couldn't use your white privilege card to get invited to the Black Lives Matter's all-black Memorial Day celebration."

Durden's comment indicates the movement is now trying to enforce the same exclusions on whites. Durden argued it is appropriate to exclude white people from Memorial Day celebrations because, "We have gay-pride parades, we have Puerto Rican Day parades, we have all kinds of parades and days that honor individuals. We have Mother's Day, we have Father's Day, so, on Mother's Day just take your momma out, not your daddy out."[lix]

Black Lives Matter is setting back the cause of racial progress. Carlson, to his credit, pointed out as much, calling Durden "hostile," "separatist," and an "apologist" for the BLM movement in their interview before summing up her stance quite neatly: "I don't care [about] your opinions, I don't care [about] your views, your life experience, your intentions. All I care about is the way you look, something that you can't control, and on that basis alone I'm judging you and I'm hostile to you."[lx]

How about Antifa? Who are they? Where did they come from? Are they really antifascist? Antifa is short for antifascist and is a far-left group. This writer views them as useful idiots promoting the Democratic Party platform. The group doesn't have an official leader or headquarters, although groups in certain states hold regular meetings. Antifa can be traced to Nazi Germany and Anti-Fascist Action, a militant group founded in the 1980s in the United Kingdom.

Much like the Socialist Party and progressive Democrats today, Antifa members support oppressed populations and protest the amassing of wealth by corporations and elites, employing radical or militant tactics to share their worldview. The socialist agenda and the deceit and deception of the one-world order movement have been woven through Antifa, who are often highly visible at so-called progressive movement rallies. The easily visible Antifa members dress head to toe in black. Members call this the "Black Bloc." In cowardly fashion they wear masks to hide their identities from the police and whomever they are protesting. The group of street thugs is well known for public and private property damage during protests. Black-clad protesters wearing masks threw Molotov cocktails and smashed windows at the University of

California Berkeley Student Union Center protesting a conservative speaker, Milo Yiannopoulos.

In his book *The Big Lie,* conservative author Dinesh

D'Souza reports hundreds of masked resisters showed up at the

University of California trying to prevent Yiannopoulos, who was a

Trump supporter, from speaking. Poor Milo, having no association

with Nazism or fascism, is vilified for stating Islam treats women

and homosexuals poorly, which is an easily observed truth.[lxi] Milo

is homosexual himself; he understands how poorly he'd be treated

under Islamic government. He'd be thrown off a burning building

or stuffed in a cage and lit on fire. Yet, the left tries to silence him.

The Nazis would not have treated him any better. These so-called

antifascist social justice warriors are soldier scammers and street-

wise political fraudsters that look and act more like fascists and

Nazis. Beware the Social Justice Warrior.

Chapter Eight
The Case of the Complicit Conniver

Everything else illusion
Adding to the confusion of the way we connive
At being alive. Tracing a line till we can define
The thing that allows us to feel. Only love is real.
— Carole King —

Have you been thinking about the supreme scammer? I've mentioned him several times. Don't envision a creepy, evil, and maybe even violent-looking thing with horns or something. That's the world's view of what Beelzebub might look like. In reality, however, I don't know what the supreme scammer looks like—and neither does Bill, Hill, or Barry O. Even Sugar Daddy Super Scammer George Soros doesn't know. Instead, the supreme scammer's powers are far greater than any super scamming socialist known to man. He's the original shape-shifting community organizer and he is an accuser, great deceiver, and goes by many names. He is not as powerful as our Creator, nor is he eternal like him; someday, the supreme scammer's power will come to an end.

In the meantime, he'll convince you with his confidence scheme as he masquerades as an angel of light.

Hidden in plain sight, The Coexist Conspiracy is the greatest conspiracy story ever told. As an old soldier and chess enthusiast, I try to recognize my opponent's battle strategy and the moves they choose to take. During the course of reviewing each case study, I trust you too have developed some sophistication in recognizing, naming, and understanding the subtleties of common deceitful tactics of the world's scammers.

As with the basic scams and rip-offs discussed earlier, the supreme scammer deceives us with many false and empty promises. Most of these promises relate to what I like to call the Honey Hoax. The obvious lie that we will be happier and more fulfilled if we sign on to the scam and deny the obvious truth right in front of us for everybody to see. Whatever passing pleasures come with the scam, they are in fact just passing. Great suffering eventually comes with almost all scams and schemes, and it surely will with this the Supreme Scam. Despite our overall self-proclaimed enlightenment, we human beings remain very gullible. We seem to love empty promises and put all sorts of false hopes in them.

Lying, cheating, stealing, and skillfully beguiling, the supreme scammer deceives his mark by weaving all sorts of complexities, creating a controlled confusion as he moves like a snake in the grass to change his victim's thinking. He is always seeking to confuse and conceal the fundamentals of the scam. Unfortunately, a sucker's mind seeks to indulge complexity as a way of avoiding the truth and making excuses. It's simple willful ignorance.

Think back again to the imagined Babel preconstruction meeting and Mr. Abaddon, the project manager. He was a nice guy; Mr. Belial, the general contractor, was his golfing buddy, and nobody was really paying attention at the previous meetings because in the end, they all knew what they wanted. They wanted unity and humanity, and not to complete the original project to have filled the Earth as they were instructed. That gig sounded like too much work. Mr. Abaddon knew from the beginning how he would beguile these easy marks because he knew human nature and what they wanted, and it was their inherent dishonesty making them such easy marks.

The supreme scammer is a *wicked-good* wordsmith. "Wicked-good" is a dualistic term used from Boston to Bangor. *Wicked* is basically a New England term. I only used it here because the supreme scammer has been called the "wicked one" by some as he skillfully twists, turns words inside out, or just plain makes them up. The dismemberment and murder of a child through abortion and sale and distribution of its body parts becomes "reproductive freedom" or "choice." Sodomy is called being "gay." When old Gabe was a kid, gay just meant you were happy. Fornication is called "cohabitation." The redefinition of marriage as it's been known for some 5,000 years is labeled "marriage freedom."

110

The supreme scammer exaggerates, falsely labels, and outright lies. Information is not the same as truth, and in today's instant-information, computer-driven world, data can be assembled very craftily to make deceitful points. One could say you and I are doing the same thing with this essay. But, I wouldn't. Certain facts and figures can be emphasized, in exclusion to others, balancing truths; and even data, which are true in themselves, become a form of honey-coated deception. Imagine?

Freedom of speech and having an honest media are essential to the American way of life. But the government-controlled media far too often resembles the same sky-screaming, rainbow-colored fist-shaking so-called progressives they are in cahoots with. In his book *Freedom From Speech*, Greg Lukianoff asserts, "As global populations increasingly expect not just physical comfort but also intellectual comfort, threats to freedom of speech are only going to become more intense. To fight back, we must understand this trend and see how students and average citizens alike are increasingly demanding freedom from speech."[lxii]

Mr. Lukianoff, of course, is referring to what today is known as hate speech. Hate speech is defined as speech expressing hatred of a particular group of people.[lxiii] The definition has been clarified by the left as any abusive or threatening speech or writing that expresses prejudice against a particular group, especially on the basis of race, religion, or sexual orientation. According to Brandi Miller, a campus minister and justice program director from the Pacific Northwest whose opinions on this matter are also embraced by her students, "Hate speech and harassment are not neutral or something that we can 'agree to disagree on.' We aren't talking about opinions on ice cream flavors, we are talking about xenophobia and racism that impacts the day to day experiences of people of color rooted in historic mothering and explicit racism."[lxiv]

I'm sorry, Professor Miller. As much as this writer finds abusive, threatening, and hateful speech abhorrent, we are going to have to agree to disagree. The Supreme Court unanimously agreed; there is no hate speech exception to the First Amendment.[lxv]

The government-controlled media and other sources of news and information often exercise their greatest power in what they do *not* report.

This tactic conveniently widens the path to destruction. Do not believe everything you think or hear. Remain sober, and seek to verify what you hear and square it with the truth. Limousine Liberals and the Fraudulent Financier are bankrolling The Coexist Conspiracy. The nation's newspapers, television networks, and cable providers are all in on the racket, which sets up an even more evil and existential scam. Beware the Complicit Conniver.

Chapter Nine
The Case of the Unexceptional American

Born down in a dead man's town
The first kick I took was when I hit the ground
End up like a dog that's been beat too much
Till you spend half your life just covering up
Born in the USA, I was born in the USA.
— *Bruce Springsteen* —

Before we begin this case study, please understand how painful it is for me to speak poorly of my country. I have always held a personal belief there is a certain level of respect and reverence that one should have for America and I always considered us exceptional, until now.

America is not OK. The coexist conspiracy fostered by the entrenched secular humanism and modernism is corrupt and oppressive. The United States was formed and once stood on the foundation of the Judeo-Christian ethic. Our foundation is crumbling—even in the Church, the foundation is

115

crumbling—and being replaced by man's word. The US continues to boast that it is exceptional because we are a nation "of the people and by the people." Following that line of thought, the US never was and never will be exceptional in relationship to its Creator. It's a nation of plain people breaking the law, making mistakes, and we are now leading the world shaking our unity and humanity rainbow-colored fists at our Creator.

Let's face it . . . the world is changing very quickly. Today in mankind's never-ending search for unity and humanity, men are marrying men, women are marrying women, our culture celebrates bisexual and transgender lifestyles, our nation is aborting babies late term, dismembering them and selling the body parts to the highest bidder.

You may be tapping into your recently developed investigative sophistication and discernment I mentioned earlier and asking yourself, how in hell does aborting millions of human beings, cutting them up and selling them on the open market, fit in with the coexist conspiracy? HELL is what it's all about. Here's how . . . .

The Abortion/Infanticide Deception

Recently, that cute little kid who lived in the White House with her dad, President Clinton, and her mom, Hillary, now all grown up, suggested, "Whether you fundamentally care about reproductive rights and access right, because these are not the same thing, if you care about social justice or economic justice, agency – you have to care about this."

She added, "It is not a disconnected fact . . . that American women entering the labor force from 1973 to 2009 added three and a half trillion dollars to our economy. Right? The net, new entrance of women—that is not disconnected from the fact that Roe became the law of the land in January of 1973."[lxvi]

Not long ago, militant femmes were protesting on the National Mall in Washington, DC, wearing the now infamous pink pussy hats as they twirled umbrellas shaped like nipples, all while screaming, "Build a uterine wall!" and waving defiant posters that boasted: "I DON'T REGRET MY ABORTION." Just recently, New York's governor, Andrew Cuomo, directed the World Trade Center's spire be lit in bright pink to celebrate his successful effort to legalize abortion up until the moment of birth. Pro-lifers pointed out his towering hypocrisy. "You lit the spire to celebrate the abortion of the unborn in the same location where I went to weep over the memorial of 11 UNBORN children killed by terrorists," tweeted pro-life activist Obianuju Ekeocha. "You memorialize the lives of those killed by terrorists, but turn around to celebrate those killed by abortionists," she declared.[lxvii]

Last fall, actress Martha Plimpton bragged publicly that her first and "best" abortion, was one she had done at a Seattle Planned Parenthood. Plimpton promotes a website and movement to #ShoutYourAbortion. Adoring fans cheered and laughed as she assured them it was "heads and tails above the rest" of her multiple abortions. "If I could Yelp review it," she cracked, "I totally would."[lxviii]

How about actress Michelle Wolf, on national television, dressed in her red, white, and blue marching band drum major costume and marching to a parade tune pontificating the sacrament of liberalism by claiming, "Look, access to abortion is good and important." She continued, "Some people say abortion is 'killing a baby.' It's not. It's stopping a baby from happening. It's like *Back to the Future* and abortion is the DeLorean."[lxix]

Pastor John McArthur asserts, "The two greatest attacks of terror on America were perpetrated by the Supreme Court. Not by any Muslim, but by the Supreme Court of the United States. The first one was the legalizing of abortion. Subsequent to that, there have been millions of babies slaughtered in the wombs of their mothers. It's incalculable to even comprehend. The blood of those lives cries out from the ground for divine vengeance on this nation."[lxx]

Continuing to ensure a thorough political and theological investigation, this detective of deception continues with an investigative pursuit of a historical understanding as it applies to unexceptional Americanism and its role in the coexist conspiracy. Clear-cut evidence has been provided by a California-based anti-abortion organization when they published a video featuring undercover footage, on-camera interviews, and a CNN appearance from Center for Medical Progress leader David Daleiden accusing Planned Parenthood of altering its abortion procedure to acquire intact fetuses to make a good sale as a matter of standard operating procedure. The video "contains heartrending admissions about the absolute barbarism of Planned Parenthood's abortion practice and baby parts sales in which fetuses are sometimes delivered intact and alive,"[lxxi] Daleiden said in a statement.

"Planned Parenthood is a criminal organization from the top down and should be immediately stripped of taxpayer funding and prosecuted for their atrocities against humanity."[lxxii]

Planned Parenthood's founder, Margaret Sanger (1879–1966), a long-time advocate for artificial birth control who supported eugenics—selective breeding and sterilization to diminish the so-called inferior races and promote the growth of so-called superior races—was the founder of the American Birth Control League (ABCL). The ABCL eventually was merged with another group, the Birth Control Clinical Research Bureau, in 1939, and was renamed the Planned Parenthood Federation of America (PPFA) in 1942. In 1952, Sanger helped found the International Planned Parenthood Federation and served as its first president until 1959.[lxxiii]

Planned Parenthood is America's largest abortion provider.[lxxiv] According to its latest annual report, Planned

Parenthood performed 327,653 abortions in 2013–14, and the organization received $528.4 million in taxpayer funding through government health service grants and reimbursements. The supreme scammer's hidden plan has been exposed. Fox News has produced and aired this EXTREMELY disturbing report that comes with a warning because it is so graphic. This writer has not been so sickened by humanity since watching the graphic black-and-white videos released by the President Dwight David Eisenhower administration after World War II.

Are you asking yourself how can this horror get worse? It can; it has clearly infected even the bones of some of the world's churches. Some ordained ministers are throwing their support behind abortion providers. Recently, for example, clergy for Episcopal and Methodist churches were among religious leaders who gathered in Cleveland to bless an abortion clinic. "I'm here today standing alongside my fellow clergymen and clergywomen to say: thank God for abortion providers," said Rev. Harry Knox,[lxxv] president and CEO of Religious Coalition for Reproductive Choice (RCRC), which supports abortion rights and what it refers to as "abortion care." Knox, who is in a same-sex marriage, was the founding director of the Human Rights Campaign's Religion and Faith Program, the first program director at Freedom to Marry, and executive director of Georgia Equality.[lxxvi] May God have mercy on us for the PURE EVIL being sold to Americans by our own Supreme Court and Planned Parenthood!

The Marriage Scam

As of 1 January 2019, same-sex marriage is legally performed and recognized in twenty-nine enlightened, smarter, we-like-our-manmade-bricks-better-than-our-Creator countries throughout the world, as of this writing. It should not be surprising that once gay marriage was declared legal, people not buying into the whole social construct of it all and who are opposed to it are now seen as enemies of the law.

This is why, especially since the Supreme Court ruled on same-sex marriage, those with moral and religious objections to same-sex marriage are increasingly being persecuted for simply following their deeply held religious convictions. Religious adoption agencies are being forced to close if they will not place children into same-sex households. Christian schools are being threatened with loss of accreditation if they do not allow their students to actively engage in homosexual practices.[lxxvii]

Professionals in the wedding industry, and even pizza shops, are being forced to participate in same-sex ceremonies or face financial ruin. Former Atlanta Fire Chief Kelvin Cochran was bullied out of his career for opposing gay marriage. Cochran was fired after he wrote a book in which he declared homosexuality and having multiple sexual partners "vile," "vulgar," and "inappropriate."[lxxviii]

Kim Davis was sent to jail because her convictions would not allow her to sign a same-sex marriage license.[lxxix] And we've only seen the beginning of this tidal wave. All of the transgender lunacy we're now facing is a result of this moral revolution as well.

Clearly, gay marriage advocates want more than the freedom to do as they please. For thousands of years, mankind has believed homosexuality is not "normal" and is inconsistent with the natural order and creation. Gay Gestapo bullies want to force everyone to either join them or they intend to destroy you and your way of life. Same-sex advocates talk a lot about love, but they have no clue what real love is. Real love "does not rejoice at wrongdoing, but rejoices with the truth."[lxxx]

The fact that many children require adoption means they are already in an undesirable situation. Their own parents ideally should be raising their children; however, a traditional married couple, as opposed to a single parent or a same-sex couple, should raise those requiring adoption. Same-sex parenting denies the child the ability to have a mom and a dad. Advocates of same-sex marriage believe parents of the same gender should be just as good as having one's own mother and father. This simply isn't true. Advocates of same-sex marriage are primarily concerned with their own perceived needs, not the needs of society as a whole or the interest of the children they adopt. Marriage is a lifelong, exclusive, traditional union of a man and a woman forming the foundation for the family. Marriage, is designed by our Creator for producing and raising children, male and female, to complement one another, and the production of children requires both a man and a woman. Gay marriage is a scam, because marriage requires a husband and a wife.

Earlier in our investigation we learned, according to the field of psychology, *cognitive dissonance* is the mental discomfort or psychological stress experienced by a person who simultaneously holds two or more contradictory beliefs, ideas, or values. Here's the latest lack of cognitive dissonance of the "Unexceptional

American"; he and she now embrace the LGBTQ, gender neutrality groupthink as settled science. In an April 2018 issue of *The Cut*, Alex Morris explores the idea of raising babies who are "theybies": neither boy nor girl. As the "theybe" grows, the baby will determine his or her own gender, choose it when the baby wants, and then live that way—at which point, the parents will go along. It's like the delusion that sex is inborn, but gender is a social construct and a sick and twisted form of deception designed to eradicate patriarchy through gender neutrality, or at the very least, create confusion, further turning mankind against itself.

Identity Fraud

The latest supreme scam of socially constructed insanity is the LGBTQ community and the entire self-identity movement; cross-dressing that is done in order to deceive, or to present oneself as something that he/she is not.

In other words, a woman changing her dress and appearance so as to appear to be a man, or a man changing his dress and appearance so as to appear to be a woman, is mental illness. The American Psychological Association (APA), The American Medical Association (AMA), and the government have bought into the scam.

According to the American Psychological Association, the LGBTQ community-organizing efforts center on the acceptance and rights of persons who identify as LGBT or queer due to centuries of persecution by church, state, and medical authorities. The APA asserts law or traditional custom banned homosexual activity or deviance from established gender roles and dress in the past, and they contend such condemnation might be communicated through sensational public trials, exile, medical warnings, and language from the pulpit today. This investigator doesn't doubt that claim for a minute.[lxxxi]

What people don't get is why liberals and leftists are always defending Islam? In fact, they have nothing but scorn for people who oppose the LGBTQ agenda. Muslims oppose the LGBTQ agenda to the point, in many Islamic countries, of the killing of gays.

Feminists attack Christianity for its patriarchy and alleged mistreatment of women. Yet, Islam treats women far worse than anything seen in the American culture. Similarly, Muslims in general support traditional sexual morality and oppose abortion. Islamic countries would likely punish the leftists who are agreeing with them for their secularism and unbelief.

When a terrorist turns out to be a Muslim, those on the left make a point of saying that we shouldn't blame all Muslims, which is true. This investigation reveals the countries ruled by Islam and its religion of works hate and death are following Islamic Sharia Law. The killing gays by throwing off buildings while family are forced to watch or stuffing your misunderstood daughter into a cage and lighting it on fire because she who wants to dress like a man into a cage they are merely compliance with fundamental Islam.

Stupid is as stupid does. The LGBTQ community and the Unexceptional American, despite all the evidence otherwise, want to believe all religions are the same and willfully ignore the truth about the differences. They have been super-scammed. They would rather believe the wisdom of the world's synthetic stone—and adopt language such as genderqueer, also known as non-binary—as a catch-all category for gender identities that are not exclusively masculine or feminine, than believe the scientific truth. Ugh!

The War Racket

The Unexceptional American is also ever-present in America's continuous involvement in war. He's wicked good at it. The United States has found itself in an endless series of wars over the past two decades. Despite frequent opposition by the party not controlling the presidency, and often the American public, the foreign policy elites operate on a consensus that routinely leads to the use of military power to solve international crises.

General Smedley D. Butler, author of the infamous book *War Is A Racket*, after a lifetime of soldiering, questioned why wars are being fought and who is benefiting from them. It is possibly the oldest and easily the most profitable, and surely the most vicious scam, con, racket, and fraud that mankind has brought on itself so willingly.

Blowing people to pieces during war is not the only scam measured by profits and killing. Murdering little babies on their birthday as they are now allowed to do in New York State is good for the economy too.

The Supreme Scammer loves war. He has trained the Unexceptional American to glorify and memorialize war and warriors on his behalf and he enjoys watching it; he's good at it and he's had a lot of practice. "From the halls of Montezuma to the shores of Tripoli we fight our country's battles in the air, on land, and sea." The Unexceptional American has had a lot of practice too, and has been involved in a major war since the country's beginning.

Smedley defined a racket as something that is NOT what it seems to be. He contended only a small "inside" group knows what it is about. It is conducted for the benefit of the very few, at the expense of the very many. From war to government-sponsored infanticide, the global elites and the Unexceptional American are making a bloody fortune.

The Environmental Racket

> *Save the trees, save the bees, save the whales, save those snails.*
> *And the greatest arrogance of all: save the planet."*
> *— George Carlin —*

Comedian George Carlin first performed his Hippie Dippie Weatherman routine on *The Ed Sullivan Show* in 1967. It was a hoot. He went on to become a social critic and philosopher known for his dark comedy and reflections on politics, language, psychology, and religion. In the early '70s, he changed his comedy routine and grew his hair long, sporting a ponytail and a beard. George was also known as the guy who got arrested with Lenny Bruce the night Bruce did his crude "Moses and Jesus" bit.[lxxxii] The whole "Imagine" baby boomer generation adopted George as their own funny rebel philosopher, even though he wasn't a baby boomer himself, being born pre-World War II in 1937. He passed away in 2008.

Believe it or not, George influenced the thinking of a whole generation of Hippie Dippie baby boomers. It's obvious George had his influence on me, because I included his work in this essay knowing how his comedic and philosophical views of the planet, environment, and humanity's impact on it depart from the liberal progressive left of today. George's whole schtick was pointing out the hypocrisy of everything and everybody. He told the truth, as he saw it. George Carlin never bought into the whole assertion the planet is in existential trouble because of humanity.

This investigation has proved so far that the past is in fact prologue. Let's take a quick look at a couple of pre-global-warming concerns with a couple recent known environmental scams.

Scientific understanding of the dangers of asbestos is well over a century old. In 1900, a London doctor discovered asbestos fibers in the lungs of a textile factory worker who died at the age of 33 from severe pulmonary fibrosis, leading the physician to believe asbestos was the cause of death. By 1918, the U.S. Bureau of Labor Statistics noticed a growing number of unusual deaths for those who worked with asbestos. By the early 1930s, a name was given to the disease, asbestosis, for those who died after being exposed to asbestos on the job. Here in America, litigation related to asbestos injuries and property damage has been claimed to be the longest-running mass tort in US history.[lxxxiii] Since asbestos-related disease was identified by the medical profession in the late 1920s, workers' compensation cases were filed and resolved in secrecy, with a flood of litigation starting in the United States in the 1970s and culminating in the 1980s and 1990s.[lxxxiv]

In the early days of the environmental asbestos abatement angle, the conventional wisdom was that it should be completely removed from buildings and schools. This was pure overreaction; people were thinking of asbestos as if it was radioactive . . . even having it near their children was unacceptable. It was the first social construct of environmental insanity and delusional belief this writer ever witnessed. What was the end result? you ask. This controlled confusion of removal increased the problem, as the dangerous, hard-to-control asbestos dust got into literally everything.

Only in the cases of renovation or demolition should removal be considered a reasonable option. Today, generally we seal or encapsulate the asbestos so that it cannot release fibers into the atmosphere. Panicking politicians without adequate scientific input started pushing through laws. Earlier, we saw that the medical profession, during the 1920s, had identified asbestos-related disease and workers' compensation cases were filed and resolved in secrecy. Environmental activists and their political allies fueled the asbestos removal scam and craziness.[lxxxv]

Do you remember Super Scammer Saul Alinsky's *Rules for Radicals*? Rule #8 states, "Keep the pressure on. Never let up." Saul's boss, the Supreme Scammer, insists on trying new scams, shams, rackets, and cons to keep the world off balance. This environmental racket is part and parcel of the overall unity and humanity scam to harness the world's people and wealth. If the opposition masters one approach, hit them from another angle with a new scam.

Nearly fifty years ago, about the same time the panicking politicians were pushing through environmental legislation on both state and federal levels quicker than one could say *Rules for Radicals #8,* John Lennon was also imagining a future utopian one-world government. Millions were participating in the first Earth Day on April 22, 1970. Portland High School, where I was a student at the time, along with colleges and universities across America, paused their anti-war protests to rally instead against pollution and population growth. The environment was now on a political par with motherhood; after all, she is called "Mother Earth."

The first Earth Day was the brainchild of Gaylord Nelson, the liberally progressive Democrat senator from Wisconsin. Senator Nelson had proposed a national "teach-in" on the environment in September 1969. This inaugural event provoked apocalyptic predictions threatening mankind's unity and humanity. "We have about five more years at the outside to do something," ecologist Kenneth Watt declared to a Swarthmore College audience on April 19, 1970. "If present trends continue, the world will be about four degrees colder for the global mean temperature in 1990, but eleven degrees colder in the year 2000," Watt declared. "This is about twice what it would take to put us into an ice age."[lxxxvi]

Apparently, Watt didn't know WHAT he was talking about! Several years later, NASA was testifying before Congress stating the world was dramatically *warming* due to manmade carbon dioxide emissions. Nearly fifty years later, the world hasn't come to an end. It hasn't frozen us to death or fried us like eggs on the sidewalk. As our case study of the "Environmental Racket" draws to a close, let us again draw from the wisdom of the late philosopher and Hippie Dippie Weatherman George Carlin.

Today's latest environmental scam is a honey of a hoax with its sweet-tasting name, The Green New Deal, and it will be a disaster. It is pure communism and it includes Medicare for all, a single-payer, government-run healthcare system demanding the government provide all the necessities desired by the delusional dreamer, pursued by the organizing scheme.

The plan provides a basic income to everybody in the one-world system, including those that choose not to work. The Green New Deal will provide public pre-k education to college. This honey of a hoax wants to ban all meat consumption and end use of all fossil fuels within ten years to combat climate change. All gas-powered cars, SUVs, and trucks will be banned, as well as all airplane travel, by 2030. Every home must be rehabilitated to peak energy efficiency. The goal is to be completely powered by clean, renewable energy resulting in zero carbon emissions, primarily through alternatives such as wind and solar. [lxxxvii]

The Supreme Scammer has employed fear all through history to harness control of people's minds and bank accounts, and even their very souls. The climate catastrophe is strictly a fear campaign—well, fear and guilt—GOD FORBID I'm killing my children as I drive my car, truck, or fly on an airplane! Carbon

dioxide fills the air! It must be my fault! I must be a bad parent!
Don't you just feel the fear and guilt these delusional dreamers are
experiencing?

Patrick Moore, who is a Greenpeace co-founder and
former president of Greenpeace Canada, recently shed some light
of sanity on The Green New Deal saying,
"It is the biggest lie since people thought the Earth was at the
center of the universe. This is Galileo-type stuff. If you
remember, Galileo discovered that the sun was at the center of
the solar system and the Earth revolved around it. He was
sentenced to death by the Catholic Church, and only because he
recanted was he allowed to live in house arrest for the rest of his
life."[lxxxviii]

The government-controlled media is an echo chamber for
The Green New Deal and they are repetitively screaming fake news
of this scam. Politicians like Rep. Alexandria Ocasio-Cortez, aka
"AOC," a Democrat from New York, and Sen. Ed Markey, a

140

Democrat from Massachusetts, who drove a local ice cream truck in Malden before he landed the nice government gig in congress. Everyone knew "Mr. Frosty " Everyone knew "Mr. Frosty" back in the early seventies. Radio talk show host and author Howie Carr said of Markey, "If only he had realized his limitations, and remained in a job that matched his skills and talents, he might have made something of himself."[lxxxix]

AOC and Senator Markey rainbow like thinking they will fix everything, *like* with a wave of *like* of their unity and humanity rainbow-colored socialist wands. Ugh! AOC didn't say that but it was fun writing it anyway. What both AOC and Markey do foresee is remaking the US economy, and they hope to eliminate all US carbon emissions in the process.[xc]

The Green New Deal sounds an awful lot like of the findings drawn from the United Nations Conference on Environment & Development held in Rio de Janeiro, Brazil, back

141

in 1992. The globalists and Alinskyites attending this groupthink conference all came to the collusion humanity was at a defining moment in history, and they came away determined to use their so-called findings to address the world's perpetuation of disparities between and within nations as justification to organize a one-world-order. The final report revealed the continued deterioration of our ecosystems are resulting in worsening poverty, hunger, ill health, and illiteracy. They conclude, "Integration of environment and development concerns and greater attention to them will lead to the fulfillment of basic needs, improved living standards for all, better protected and managed ecosystems and a safer, more prosperous future. No nation can achieve this on its own; but together we can - in a global partnership for sustainable development." "Integration of the environment" and "No nation can achieve this on their own" sounds a lot like community-organizing the world.[xci]

And moreover, this miracle transformation must take place within a decade. Why? Because AOC claims there's a scientific consensus that, unless drastic action is taken, the planet has only 12 years before it is destroyed by climate change. She says it is her generation's "World War II"—a life-death struggle against the forces of darkness. Call it the coming green apocalypse. It is nonsense, environmentalist hysteria masquerading as science.

Like George, I too am tired of Earth Day. I'm tired of global cooling and global warming. I'm tired of asbestos scams. I'm tired of seeing legit compensation claims threatened or made less by scams and fraud. Mostly, I'm tired of these soldier scammers, social justice warriors, environmental activists, and yes, as George so eloquently said, "Tired of white, bourgeois liberals who think the only thing wrong with this country is there aren't enough bicycle paths."[xcii]

Philosopher and Hippie Dippie Weatherman George philosophizes,[xciii] "Did you ever think about the arithmetic? The planet has been here four and a half billion years. We've been here, what, a hundred thousand? Maybe two hundred thousand years? And we've only been engaged in heavy industry for a little over two hundred years two hundred years versus four and a half billion. And we have the CONCEIT to think that somehow we're a threat?"

The Collaborating Coup

As I mentioned in the beginning, I have always held a personal belief there is a certain level of respect and reverence every citizen should have for America. I've always considered myself a patriot due to my love for my country and have believed it be an exceptional nation among nations. The American citizen of my generation remembers from his high school civic studies the Declaration of Independence taught us that the founding principle of America is "*We hold these truths to be self-evident, that all men are created equal, that re Life Liberty and the pursuit of happiness."* That is an exceptional idea!

This investigation has confirmed America has been a major world military and economic power since the end of World War II. During that time, this nation has been both positively and negatively influencing the rest of the world with its military and economic power. Today, America, like many other nations, is falling victim to a supreme scam spreading the Earth. The scam, we determined earlier, is The Coexist Conspiracy, which is being thrust on the world's inhabitants by global elites in an effort to convince America and the world that to eliminate war, violence, hatred, and have a fair distribution of the world's wealth and resources; we must pursue a new, improved, supersized one-world order.

The Unexceptional American and the world at large have been unable find a way to run an independent nation-state without scamming each other—so how could humanity possibly do it for the world? The truth is, America and the world isn't wrestling against just flesh and blood people, we are fighting against wickedness in very high places. From my dear friend Art getting driveway sealer scammed in Portland, Maine, to the now certified coup attempt to overthrow a duly elected president of the United States, we can clearly see the great deceiver and accuser who is a supreme scammer has been behind it all.

Most American baby boomers, now called senior citizens, were required to take a high school civics course during high school where they learned that the supreme power of our nation is held by the people themselves and our elected representatives instead of a totalitarian government so prevalent throughout the rest of the world. The sad reality is, the Unexceptional American knows little about their-own Constitution, Bill of Rights, or the function of their own American government. The Department of Education and American Teachers Union-sponsored ignorance paved the way for the now conspiratorial network of evil socialist power operating independently of America's current president in pursuit of their own one-world order within the government itself. In 1976, President James Earl Carter, the progressive, pro-Palestinian, anti-Israel, socialist-leaning Democrat, sold his soul in an effort to receive the endorsement of the largest labor union in the United States—the National Education Association (NEA).[xciv] Only three years after his inauguration the unpopular president, who was running for a second term, created the Department of Education for the federal government to "meet its responsibilities in education more effectively, more efficiently, and more responsively."[xcv] This investigator of indoctrinating institutions has determined the Department of Education is now part of the scam.

The Department of Education has grown enormously alongside other bloated departments of government loaded with entrenched federal employees furthering their government-sanctioned union interests, not taxpayer, by voting for the comforting lies put forth by the supreme scam. These civil servants are simply useful idiots who got all caught up in the woven web of deceit and deception. However, there are those in the government unions and other well-established civil servants of deception who are actively working against the current administration, obstructing, resisting, and subverting its policies and directives. They are the soldier scammers. This old detective of cunning and collaborating communists remembers Boris Badenov lookalike Russian communist leader Nikita Khrushchev, who boldly stated in 1956, "We will take America without firing a shot. We do not have to invade the U.S. We will destroy you from within...."[xcvi] I remember thinking "That will never happen." And now I am sad to see Khrushchev's words coming true.

It doesn't take Sherlock's magnifying glass to see the continuity of government itself, job security for its union members and the pursuit of unity and humanity by globalists are all woven together using the existing fabric of corrupt government working the supreme scam.

This detective of dumbed-downed delusional dreamers detects they are but useful idiots promoting no borders, no walls, and sanctuary for all, and are historically ignorant as they fall for the scam. The supreme scammer doesn't want independent, thinking Americans spending too much time analyzing the web of deceit. Instead, the scammer effectively used a couple of generations of dumbed-down delusional dreaming community-organizing Americans who may or may not be aware of the globalist agenda.

In fact, the globalist one-world scammers don't want well-informed, well-educated people capable of critically thinking through a problem. They want lemmings. They want people to be like those stupid little critters that follow each other jumping off a cliff to their death. They want people to just follow orders. The dealers of this diversity delusion don't want people who are educated and informed enough to see how The Coexist Conspiracy is sucking them into a one-world government system.

149

Basically, the conspiratorial web of deceit and deception within the American government wants you ignorant enough to go to work every day and accept all the lies. They want you to accept government control instead of freedom. They want you to accept same-sex marriage and transsexual drag queens reading children stories in school. They want you to remain ignorant enough to pay taxes for government-sponsored, unfettered abortion and infanticide. They want you to have the same measly pay, benefits, housing, and healthcare as everybody else. Individual accomplishments and thought will be eventually verboten. Beware the Unexceptional American.

Chapter Ten

The Case of the Naughty Nationalist

This land is your land, this land is my land
From the California to the New York island
From the Redwood Forest, to the gulf stream waters
This land was made for you and me
- Woody Guthrie -

My dear trusted sidekick and co-detective of diversity deceit and deception, let us not forget the supreme scammer is a wicked-good wordsmith. He exaggerates, falsely labels, and outright lies. As is typical with today's government-controlled media, information is not the same as truth, and in today's instant-information, computer-driven world, data can be assembled, disassembled, and reassembled very craftily to make deceitful points. I have mentioned it before; we could be accused of the same thing.

The Merriam-Webster Dictionary defines *nationalism* as 1: a loyalty and devotion to a nation *especially*: a sense of national consciousness exalting one nation above all others and placing primary emphasis on promotion of its culture and interests as opposed to those of other nations or supranational groups. 2: a nationalist movement or government.[xcvii]

A *white supremacist* they define as a person who believes the white race is inherently superior to other races and white people should have control over people of other races.[xcviii] The scammer's wordsmithing now has a fairly new twist on his scheme to create controlled confusion and point fingers using race as a tool to disassemble and then reassemble his form of unity and humanity. He has combined nationalism with racial supremacy, and threw in the increasing hatred of white people and came up with the term "White Nationalist." It has been added to Merriam-Webster Dictionary as meaning one of a group of militant whites who espouse white supremacy and

152

advocate enforced racial segregation.[xcix] Keep these terms in mind as we proceed with our political and theological inquiry into the facets of nationalism and its role in The Coexist Conspiracy.

Our investigation thus far has shown that people down through history hold an undeniable attachment to their native land. They often hang onto values of their parents, families, and ways of life from their homeland. Clearly, the supreme scammer sees the sentiment of people as an opportunity to use the deceptive unity and humanity gig once again. He *picks, personalizes,* and *polarizes* people by using racial, economic, religious, and political incitements. The supreme scammer, who is also the great accuser, uses the Alinskyite *Rules For Radicals* #13 and will *"Pick the target, freeze it, personalize it, and polarize it."* He uses any tactic that effectively cuts off the support network and isolates the target from any possible sympathy from the masses. White Nationalist is just the new term of political incitement being used to create racial tension and division.

Adolf Hitler was a lot more than a nationalist or just a person who believes their nation is superior to all others. Hitler had his own national socialists with their hateful and prideful sense of superiority rooted in the unity of their shared humanity, ethnicity, and language, which sounds an awful lot like we are back in Babel. This detective of denied diversity suspects maybe project manager Mr. Abaddon and Adolf Hitler were a lot alike, maybe went to the same schools and hung out with the same crowd. These puffed-up political pons of the perpetrating poltergeist known as the supreme scammer often focus on sharing the beguiling interests of music, literature, and of course, sports, which if woven just right, emboldens nationalism. Think about all the air force fly-overs and pregame patriotic anthems you saw at the last professional football game you attended.

Adolf Hitler's National Socialist German Worker's Party (Nazi) embraced a strict superiority hierarchy of the human race.

Hitler's view regarding race is found his book *Mein Kampf,* which was the propaganda text issued to the Hitler Youth. He spelled out in demonic detail the European races in descending order on the Nazi hierarchy. Adolf Hitler and the Nazi Party were responsible for the Holocaust and the mass murder of millions.[c]

Hitler's work in *Mein Kampf* regarding "the race of the German people" cited works of Hans F. K. Günther, a well-known German writer, eugenicist, and racist employed by the Weimar Republic and the Nazi Third Reich. Hitler made references to Günther's classifications of the Aryan race as a superior type of humanity. The purest stock of Aryans, according to Nazi ideology, were the Nordic people of Germany, England, Denmark, The Netherlands, Sweden, and Norway.[ci]

Today, the socialist-progressive political left attempts to make any disagreement with their socialist-rainbow LGBTQ, no borders, no walls, sanctuary for all agenda analogous with Hitler or the Nazi party.

I met an old friend from Massachusetts for lunch at Three Dollar Dewey's who was shopping in Portland. The current American president was on the television behind the bar. Some years earlier, I applied one of Alinsky's favorite *Rules for Radicals* myself by picking and polarizing my friend Leon as a liberal-leaning looney. He's always been looney and leaning increasingly liberal over the years, but Leon is my long-time friend and I love him anyway. I've heard Leon complain and get a little angry when discussing conservatives and the conservative thought since Ronald Reagan. I had no reason to think this conversation was going to be any different, but it was; it was very different. Leon's face was red and he was clenching his fists as he watched the president speak. This wasn't just anger, it was some sort of mental derangement syndrome that I've read about but never personally witnessed.

Leon took a sip of his beer, pounded his fist on the table and angrily asked me, *"Do you know who he is?"* Spitting his beer and

156

pointing to the TV, *"He's the 'you're fired' guy from TV. His method of operation is exactly like Hitler!"*

So being a thorough detective of political posturing, I not only decided to *pick* and *polarize* my friend Looney Leon a little, I had fun poking at his position with a preponderance of persuasive evidence to the contrary. I decided to risk it all and asked him, *"Do you know what I like about the president?"* I was prepared to provide a short list of likes and dislikes, such as finally recognizing Jerusalem as capital of Israel, or the much-improved economy as evidenced by historically thrifty friend driving to Maine to spend his Massachusetts money shopping and hopefully picking up the tab for my lunch. As for my dislikes, I would have told him about the president's puffed-up personality and salty language. I don't believe my friend even heard me, as he was still staring at the president surrounded by supporters on television. His anger was building; I thought my old friend's head was going to explode. Leon once again pounded his fist on the table and pointed to the television, saying, *"And his supporters, they're like Hitler too!"* Clearly my friend Leon's anger and emotional inability to cope with views different from his own are driving his newly aquired desire to compare those people to Hitler. This desire to accuse people of being like Hitler is known as Reductio-ad-Hitlerum. Hitler is the most universally despised figure in modern history, so any connection to him, or his beliefs, can erroneously cause others to view the argument in a similar light. It's a desperate attempt by the accuser to deny truth of a discussion point out of lack of reasonable counterargument and it is working well for the soldier scammers and one-world organizing globalist crowd. Even Pope Francis pulls out the Nazi card, referring to populist politicians, *"They sow fear and then make decisions. Fear is the beginning of dictatorships,"* he said. "Let's go back to the last century, to the fall of the Weimar Republic. I repeat this a lot. Germany needed a way out and, with promises and fears, Hitler came forward." He said all this because he one-world government globalist too.[cii]

Of course, we all know the pope's reference and Leon's assertion of the American president's "method of operation is just like Hitler's" is absurd, and it's almost as absurd as that unnamed derangement disorder. Let us never forget, Adolf Hitler and the Nazi Party were responsible for the Holocaust and the mass murder of millions.[ciii] Not puffed-up, salty patriots like the American president.

We saw earlier that just plain *nationalism* is defined as a loyalty and devotion to a nation, especially a sense of national consciousness exalting one nation above all others and placing primary emphasis on promotion of its culture and interests as opposed to those of other nations.

It's not in and of itself a bad thing to take pride in one's nation and superiority in any one discipline—do you enjoy the Olympics? Beware the Naughty Nationalist.

Chapter Eleven
The Case of the Religion Racket

Religion is the sigh of the oppressed creature,
The heart of a heartless world and the soul of soulless conditions.
It is the opium of the people.
– Karl Marx –

Once again, we need to look through Sherlock's

magnifying glass at both history and Scripture to uncover political

and theological deception. The past is definitely prologue in the

religion racket. For the purposes of this case study, we need a basic

understanding of the three general religion categories, as it is

necessary for evidential research and analysis.

Religion has been defined as a system of beliefs concerning

the cause, nature, and purpose of the universe, especially when

considered as the creation of a superhuman agency or agencies,

usually involving devotional and ritual observances and often containing a moral code of belief.[civ] This investigation will prove beyond a shadow of a doubt that the supreme scammer has used world religion to lead man away from the truth.

Religion has deceived mankind down through the ages by convincing it of the need for mankind to reach up to its Creator through religion and tradition instead of recognizing that the Creator already reached down to mankind 2,000 years ago and his work is "finished." [cv]This investigation has traced religion and its influence on civilization to its ancient Near East origin. Sometimes studying history and religion for political and theological investigation can be as unpleasant as going through the dusty and dirty cold case files located in the basement of a local precinct police station in Bangor, Maine. Taking an honest approach to studying religion is dirty and dusty too. The basement world religions are classified in three basic categories, and they are summarized as: polytheistic, pantheistic, and monotheistic.

Polytheism

Polytheism is the belief in many gods. Hinduism is believed to be the first of the polytheistic religions, and believed to have originated about 2500 BC. The Bhagavad Gita, Hindu Scripture, are where it's revealed that many gods were subject to a supreme Brahman god as the ultimate reality—one Supreme Spirit in many forms. Many ancient cultures, including Assyria, Babylonia, Greece, and Rome, were polytheistic. These belief systems viewed gods as being in control of all natural events, such as rainfall, harvests, and fertility. Generally, polytheistic cultures believed in sacrifices to appease their gods. For instance, the Canaanites sacrificed to the male god, Baal, and his female counterpart, Ashtaroth. Baal controlled the rain and the harvest, while Ashtaroth controlled fertility and reproduction. The Greeks and Romans developed polytheism to a highly structured pantheon of gods and goddesses.

Pantheism

Pantheism is the principle that god is everything, and everything is god. Therefore, nature is also part of god. We must be in harmony with nature. We must nurture it and be nurtured by it. Mankind is no different than any other animal. We must live in harmony with them, understand them, and learn from them, focusing on the relationship between mankind and the elements of nature. Pantheism is a belief that all is god. The belief in a supernatural power that organizes and animates the material universe was adopted in many ancient cultures. The belief that the universe itself was divine was typified in the beliefs of the African and American Indian cultures, the later Egyptian religion under the pharaohs, and Buddhism, Confucianism, and Taoism in the cultures of the Far East. Pantheistic beliefs are also finding resurgence.

Monotheism

Monotheism is a belief in one God. It is the foundation of the Judeo-Christian-Muslim line of religions, which began with a man named Abraham in about 2000 BC. From this point in history, God began revealing himself to the world through the nation of Israel. The Jewish Scriptures record the journey of the Israelites from slaves in Egypt to the Promised Land in Canaan under the leadership of Moses.

During a period of about 1,500 years, God revealed what became the Old Testament of the Bible, relating the history of Israel with the character and laws of God. During the period of the Roman Empire, Jesus Christ was born in Bethlehem as the long-awaited Messiah. The ministry of Jesus ended in about 32 AD with his crucifixion and resurrection. After Christ's ascension into Heaven, the Christian church grew in his name and the New Testament was written. About 600 years later, Muhammad began preaching in Mecca. Muhammad believed he was the ultimate prophet of God, and he taught Islam as recorded in the Qur'an.

Atheism is really a modern belief that resulted from the Enlightenment period of the eighteenth century. According to AmericanAtheists.org, Atheism is not a belief system. It's not a religion and it is NOT a disbelief in gods or denial of gods; it is a lack of belief in gods. That clarifies it for me. I think I get it . . . They don't believe in polytheistic, pantheistic gods or a monotheistic God. They just don't believe in the God of the Bible or any other gods.

Karl Marx believed religion is the self-consciousness and self-esteem of someone lost to themselves. He believed the state and society produced religion, which he contends, "is an inverted consciousness of the world, because they are in an inverted world."cvi Marx asserted religion is a fantastic realization of the human essence, since the human essence has not acquired any true reality.

The struggle, he clarifies for us, is indirectly linked to the struggle against the world, whose spiritual aroma is religion.[cvii]

President Barack Hussein Obama, referring to religious working-class voters in old industrial towns decimated by job losses, said, "They get bitter, they cling to guns or religion or antipathy to people who aren't like them or anti-immigrant sentiment or anti-trade sentiment as a way to explain their frustrations."[cviii]

Friedrich Wilhelm Nietzsche was a German philosopher, cultural critic, composer, poet, philologist, and Latin and Greek scholar whose work has exerted a tremendous influence on Western philosophy and modern intellectual thought. He began his career as a classical philologist.

Philology is the study of language in oral and written historical sources; it is the intersection between textual criticism, literary criticism, history, and linguistics. He later turned to philosophy, thinking about the world and the universe in more abstract ways.

Nietzsche was highly critical of the three Abrahamic religions: Judaism, Christianity, and Islam. In his book *Genealogy of Morals*, written in 1885, Nietzsche began searching their origins, shared beliefs, and values. Whoa! Nietzsche missed the forest for the trees. He believed that "good" does not refer to a natural state of being. He thought that it began as a word the nobility used simply to describe themselves and their own actions. Over time, it became used to refer directly to those individuals who had a reputation for achievement. The good doctor, the learned professor, the good lady, are expressions used not that long ago that come immediately to mind. I think today the scamming wordsmiths call this "virtue signaling," or the action or practice of publicly expressing opinions or sentiments intended to demonstrate one's good character or the moral correctness of one's position on a particular issue.

Nietzsche discussed good and bad as a natural pair of moral attributes, bad simply describing something that was not good, namely the "slaves" and their personality characteristics. He called this original moral structure master-morality. He used a French term, *ressentiment*, to describe the disdain among the unsuccessful people who were consistently referred to as bad.

Nietzsche asserted that "bad" people eventually claimed the term *goodness* for themselves, linking it with values previously associated with being bad under master-morality. Nietzsche called the resulting system slave-morality, with concepts such as humility and chastity becoming celebrated, and their opposites and the once considered "good" traits within master-morality now were deemed not only bad, but they were evil. Nietzsche considered Christianity as slave-morality, encouraging personal weakness. Nietzsche got it half-right, and I'll return to this thought later in this essay.

If Marx's view of religion as the "opium of the people" [cix]a nd President Obama's reference to fellow Americans as "bitter clingers" are taken in consideration with Nietzsche's view of Christianity as slave-morality, we can see the supreme scammer is using the world religions as a tool to community-organize the world, harnessing the people and the world's wealth for his own. The supreme scammer, who is the world's greatest deceiver, has convinced people that religion can save you. As I mentioned earlier, religion is mankind reaching up to its Creator by a self-proclaimed adherence to the beliefs and practices of a religion in the hope that performance will gain right standing with the Creator of all.

This investigation has revealed religion to be a diversionary plan and supreme scam of Lucifer to heap the burdensome observance of traditions, rites, and rituals, which get in the way of people seeing truth. Religion is a demonically inspired manmade racket!

In contrast, Christianity is not a religion! As mentioned earlier, religions are about human attempts to make our lives right with God, through our good works, sacrifices, rituals, and money. Christianity is about God entering human history to graciously save men and women through his Son, Jesus Christ. It is only by placing our faith in Jesus Christ and submitting to his Lordship that we will be saved.

The delusional dreamer and the average conniving con may not be aware who the Supreme Scammer is and where he came from, but Saul Alinsky, Bill, Hill, Barry O, and Sugar Daddy George all know who he is because in Saul Alinsky's most famous book, the 1971 *Rules for Radicals* includes a dedication to "the first radical known to man who rebelled against the establishment and did it so effectively that he at least won his own kingdom— Lucifer."

Remember what Saul said during the *Playboy* interview: "Once I get into hell, I'll start organizing the have-nots over there. When *Playboy* asked, why them?

Saul replied, "They're my kind of people." Again I ask, what kind of people are those, Saul? Demon people? Saul said Lucifer won his own kingdom—guess where that kingdom is located. Yes, you are correct, O trusted sidekick; he's talking about the world we live in. He is, in fact, the god of this world. Lucifer, more commonly known as Satan, was cast from Heaven because of pride that originated from his desire to be God instead of a servant of God. Satan was the highest of all the angels, but he wasn't happy. He desired to be God and rule the universe. God cast Lucifer out of Heaven as a fallen angel.

Satan is often humorously caricatured as a red-horned, trident-raising cartoon villain, and it's no wonder people don't believe in him. Frankly, he likes it that way. Lucifer's greatest scam is making the world believe he doesn't exist. His existence, however, is not based on fantasy. It's verified in the same ancient Scripture that narrates Jesus's life and death, the Holy Bible.

Bible-believing Christians know Lucifer is actually the world's leader of the fallen angels. These demons, existing in the invisible spirit realm yet affecting our physical world, rebelled against God, but are ultimately under his control. He masquerades as an "angel of light," some people call him the "morning star" because he goes about deceiving humans just as he deceived Adam and Eve in the beginning.

Lucifer, Satan, the devil, is also called the "prince of the power of the air."[cx] He is in fact the "ruler of this world."[cxi] These titles and many more signify Satan's capabilities. To say, for example, that Satan is the prince of the power of the air is to signify that in some way, he rules over the world and the people in it.

This is not to say that he rules the world completely; God is still sovereign. But it does mean that God, in his infinite wisdom, has allowed Satan to operate in this world within the boundaries God has set for him. When the Bible says Satan has power over the world, we must remember that God has given him domain over unbelievers only. Believers are no longer under the rule of Satan.[cxii]Unbelievers, on the other hand, are caught "in the snare of the devil"[cxiii] lie in the "power of the evil one" [cxiv]and are in bondage to Satan.[cxv]

So, when the Bible says that Satan is the "god of this world," it is not saying that he has ultimate authority. It is conveying the idea that Satan rules over the unbelieving world in a specific way. Lucifer is the god of this world and he has blinded the minds of unbelievers so they cannot see the light of the gospel of the glory of Jesus Christ. This supreme scammer includes promoting false philosophies in the world—philosophies that blind the unbeliever to the truth of the Gospel. Lucifer's philosophies are humanism, secularism, liberalism, and all the isms which are the fortresses in which people are imprisoned, and they can only be set free by the blood of Jesus Christ.

I've mentioned it before, and it's always worth

restating; the best example and most widespread of the false philosophies is the belief that man can earn God's favor by a certain act or acts. In almost every false religion, meriting God's favor or earning eternal life is a predominant theme. Earning salvation by works, however, is contrary to biblical revelation. Man cannot work to earn God's favor; eternal life is a free gift.[cxvi] And that free gift is available through Jesus Christ and him alone.

Are you asking why mankind does not simply receive the free gift of salvation? Clearly, Lucifer, Satan, or the devil—the god of this world—has tempted mankind to follow his pride instead. Satan sets the agenda, the unbelieving world follows, and mankind continues to be deceived. It is no wonder that Scripture calls Lucifer the great deceiver.

Studies tell us more Americans believe in God than believe the devil exists.[cxvii] Many believe Satan is just a fairy tale. Convincing the world he does not exist has been Satan's greatest accomplishment. But in reality, the devil is on his game like never before. The Bible says of Lucifer, "He is the one who deceives" the "ruler of demons" the "enemy," "the father of lies," and the Apostle Paul referred to Satan as "the god of this world."[cxviii]

We observed all throughout this investigation that he makes use of the world using every tool possible to harness the people and the world's wealth for himself. Lucifer is known for using the simplest of things straight through to the most complex to work his evil battle plans. From the simple driveway sealing scam that my dear old friend Art fell for to the worldwide coexist conspiracy, Supreme Scamming Lucifer's favorite projects seem to be worldly kingdoms, corrupt governments, self-serving politicians, false religions, entertainment, sex, drugs, and yes, even our own puffed-up Unexceptional American. These have all been his weapons of his spiritual war on the world and our nation, and I'm afraid the enemy is winning…at least for now.

The Bible tells us, Satan even went to the point of putting Jesus Christ to the test by tempting him using the extremes of worldly comforts. He first tempted Jesus with the basic human need of food in the form of bread after he was in the desert fasting for forty days and nights. When that didn't seem to work, he moved on to a greater temptation, or so he thought. He offered Jesus "all the kingdoms of the world and their splendor."[cxix]

Of course, Jesus answered Satan by telling him that, "Man does not live by bread alone, but on every word, that comes from the mouth of God," and, "Away from me Satan! For it is written: Worship the Lord your God, and serve him only."[cxx]

Jesus's temptation was real, and so is ours. Lucifer's battle plan is to deceive us and do it every day. He was there in the beginning watching the "fall of man"[cxxi] to his great pleasure. America and the world at large have failed to recognize the enemy because many believe Satan is just another fairy tale, but he is often hiding in their religion. This supreme scammer and great deceiver is pretending to make his way appear a more rational way and linking worldliness with Christianity. Beware the Religion Racket.

Chapter Twelve
The Case of the Intersecting Ideology

The intersection of religion and world politics
has often been a bloody crossroads.
- Elliott Abrams -

We discovered in the last case study the Supreme Scammer

is Lucifer of the Holy Bible. He is a great deceiver and has been the

one weaving the web of deceit and deception through each

previously investigated case study. He also continues to pursue

Jerusalem in an effort to set up shop declaring himself to be God.

This detective of political and theological deceit and deception is

now looking inward toward collaborating Christianity for evidence

of involvement in the design and facilitation of a false religion scam

contributing to The Coexist Conspiracy.

I suspect Lucifer's supreme scam to get Jerusalem for

himself fell mostly on unwitting Arab people, who ultimately fell

victim to one of the dastardliest swindles ever devised. The early Christian church was growing and the gospel was being spread. Many Christians were being persecuted by both the Jews and the Roman government and in 70 AD, about the time of Passover, the Roman general Titus besieged Jerusalem, thoroughly destroying the great Jewish temple, fulfilling Christ's prophecy.[cxxii] The Dome of the Rock Mosque now stands as Islam's second-most holy place where the temple once stood.

Therefore, our investigation necessitates we travel to another country on the other side of the world. We are traveling to an independent city-state encircled by a forty-foot-tall border wall. The country we are visiting is a monarchy, and is a fairly powerful member of the United Nations. It's like any other civilized society having its own flag, anthem, currency, postage stamps, passports, and license plates. I'm not talking about Israel; we're going to the Nation of Vatican City, also known as the Holy See.[cxxiii]

Once again, we need to look through Sherlock's magnifying glass to both history and Scripture to uncover political and theological deception, so let's begin by gaining an understanding of the branch of theology, the study of God, called eschatology.[cxxiv]

Strong eschatological clues highlight the globalist efforts to community-organize the world, and they rest in the end of days intersection of the three major religions: Judaism, Islam, and Christianity. Christianity, we determined in the last case study, is not a religion. However, for the purposes of this case study, we need to obtain a basic understanding of intersecting eschatological views.

Judaism believes there is one God who cannot be made up of parts. The Jews' view is, any attempt to divide God's oneness is seen as a pagan throwback to yesteryear when mankind had many gods. The Messiah in Judaism is a seen savior and liberator of the

Jewish people and is an anointed king or high priest to come. In Jewish eschatology or end times study, the Messiah is a future Jewish king from the line of David who is expected to rule the Jewish people during the world to come. The Messiah is often referred to as King Messiah.[cxxv]

Islam embraces an immaterial, invisible God, Allah—one to be intensely feared. They are looking for the return of Imam-al-Mahdi, or what we would call the Islamic Messiah.[cxxvi]

Christians hold fast to the trinity of God the Father, God the Son, and God the Holy Spirit. To Christians, God gives a revelation of himself through his flesh Son, Jesus Christ, who is God incarnate, and they look to him as the soon to return Jewish-Christian King Messiah.

These three major religions each have a holy place where they look for guidance. Large portions of early Christianity looked to the Vatican as the Holy City for religious structure and guidance. The Roman Catholic Church considers itself to be a pre-denominational church, and much of the world still looks to it that way as well. Let me point out, NO other Christian denomination precedes it. Within this denomination, there are approximately one billion, two hundred eighty-five million people making up more than half the Christians in the world.[cxxvii]

The Jews look to the Western Wall in Jerusalem, which is the most holy place accessible to the Jewish people. It is known in recent centuries as the "Wailing Wall," and was built by Herod the Great as the retaining wall of the Temple Mount complex. The plaza was created as an area for prayer when Israel captured the Old City in 1967. Thousands of people gather here for prayer.[cxxviii]

The Muslims look to Mecca as their Holy City. Mecca is a city in western Saudi Arabia in the Sirat Mountains, inland from the Red Sea coast. It is the holiest of Muslim cities. Muhammad, the founder of Islam, was born in Mecca, and it is toward this location that Muslims turn five times daily in prayer. All devout Muslims attempt to go to Mecca at least once in their lifetime, because it is believed to be sacred, and only Muslims are allowed to enter the city.

Each religious group believes that they receive certain types of blessings for the rest of their lives for visiting their holy place. In the beginning, Arab visitors would bring gifts to the House of God, and the keepers of the Kaaba were gracious to all who came. Some brought their idols and, not wanting to offend these people, their idols were placed inside the sanctuary. It is said that the Jews looked upon the Kaaba as an outlying tabernacle of the Lord with veneration until it became polluted with idols. The offerings were dumped into the well and it was filled with sand. Years later, Abd Al-Muttalib reported he had visions telling him where to find the well and its treasure.[cxxix] He became the hero of Mecca, and destined to become the grandfather of Muhammad.

Grandfather Abdul-Muttalib took it upon himself to raise Mohammad and when he died, Mohammad's kind uncle immediately took him in despite his own poverty. Abu Talib's loyalty to Muhammad did not waver before, during, or after the Prophet's revelation. Abu Talib said he concealed his beliefs so that he could play as a mediator between the Prophet and the other chiefs of Mecca who refused the idea of the new religion. If it wasn't for Abu Talib's service, the Messenger of Allah could not have converted the idol worshipper Arabs. Uncle Abu Talib took young Muhammad on a business trip/trade caravan to Syria and while in a place called Bursa,[cxxx] a Roman Catholic monk[cxxxi] learned of his identity and said, "Take your brother's son back to his country and guard him against the Jews, for by god, if they see him and know of him that which I know, they will construe evil against him. Great things are in store for this brother's son of yours."

Jerusalem is a "cup of trembling,"[cxxxii] and has always been in a constant state of turmoil. It has been conquered many times, and was under Islamic rule for many centuries since the time of Christ. Rome too was sacked a few times, but it has never experienced the constant turmoil of Jerusalem, "The City of Peace."[cxxxiii] I believe the Supreme Scammer Lucifer facilitated moving the Church to Rome away from the Middle East during the first generation after Christ.

Non-religious Christians who preached the pure gospel suffered persecution and were squeezed between Roman Catholicism and Islam. Both were growing in power, but would not tolerate opposition.[cxxxiv] This political and theological detective of dastardly deeds believes the Vatican initially collaborated and encouraged Islam during its beginning and is once again doing so with the same goal.

The Vatican, which is visibly filled with the wealth and spoils of its own attempt at world domination, is now a fully recognized country in the world and voting member of the United Nations. This detective of deception contends that Lucifer, the great deceiver and supreme scammer, has manipulated the Vatican and the papacy, facilitating the growth of Islam way back in

600 AD as a false religion, a scam and racket to harness the Arab people and their wealth for unity and humanity. Lucifer has set up Muhammad as a leader for the Arabs, who are the children of Ishmael, to follow raising him up as a great leader whom he could control and eventually unite all the non-Catholic Arabs. I suspect the pope was planning the Crusades to come if necessary, creating a mighty army that would ultimately capture Jerusalem and set up shop for his papal view of unity and humanity.

There is nothing new under the sun. In his own words, Pope Francis said of his pilgrimage to the United Arab Emirates, a "new page in the history of the dialogue between Christianity and Islam" and in promoting world peace based on brotherhood. The pope and the grand imam signed the landmark document titled "Human Fraternity for World Peace and Living Together," which says it is "a document on a human fraternity for world peace and living together."[cxxxv] He called upon the world's "intellectuals, philosophers, religious figures, artists, media professionals and men and women of culture in every part of the world, to rediscover the values of peace, justice, goodness, beauty, human fraternity and coexistence in order to confirm the importance of these values as anchors of salvation for all, and to promote them everywhere."[cxxxvi]

For political and theological study's sake, let's say the Vatican wanted Muhammad for an Arab leader. Let's also float the idea that with the right instruction and teaching, Muhammad could unite all the non-Catholic Arabs behind him, creating an army mighty enough that it could capture Jerusalem.

Not so many years ago, at a National Prayer Breakfast, following his condemnation of ISIS violence, former President Barack Hussein Obama had this to say: "Humanity has been grappling with these questions throughout human history. And lest we get on our high horse and think this is unique to some other place, remember that during the Crusades and the Inquisition, people committed terrible deeds in the name of Christ."[cxxxvii]

Remember what Super Scammer Saul Alinsky said in his book *Rules for Radicals* #8, "*Keep the pressure on. Never let up.*"[cxxxviii] **He and the last four hundred years of Islamic apologists have been hammering the sins of the Crusades as some sort of twisted defense for the current sins of Islam.**

The truth is, during the Crusades and Inquisition, people did terrible things that no Christian should do or should defend. The Crusades and military expositions were organized by Rome and western European Christians in response to centuries of Islamic expansion and war. The objective was control of Europe and the Holy Land and to conquer pagan areas, all with the ultimate goal to recapture formerly Christian territories. Crusading and papal authority declined rapidly in Europe and the Middle East during the sixteenth century as the Protestant Reformation grew.

Let's return again to young Muhammad a few centuries earlier, who married a wealthy Arabian lady named Khadijah. She was a devout Roman Catholic,[cxxxix] and I suspect she may have been used by the Vatican for more than her money, which she reportedly gave to the pope liberally. Khadijah had a cousin named Waraquah, who was also a very faithful Roman Catholic. Khadījah provided instrumental support in Muhammad's early days as the coming false prophet. Her wealth allowed him the leisure to meditate, and like a supportive wife, I expect she reassured him of the authenticity of his revelations. Kadijah's cousin Waraquah, who was also a devout Roman Catholic, is said to have likened Muhammad's revelations to those of Moses, further providing Muhammad confidence in his revelations.[cxl] He had tremendous influence on Muhammad. Teachers were sent to young Muhammad and he had intensive training.

Muhammad began receiving so-called divine revelations and his wife's Catholic cousin, Waraquah, assisted in interpreting. From joint effort came the Qur'an. Muhammad later conquered Mecca and cleared the Kaaba of idols.[cxli] History proves that before

Islam came into existence, people in Arabia worshiped the moon-god, who was married to the sun god.

In their holy book, the Qur'an, Christ is regarded as a mere prophet. If the pope was Christ's representative on Earth, then he also must be a prophet of God. This may have caused the followers of Muhammad to fear and respect the pope as a holy man, as Islam does to this very day.[cxlii]

As time went by, the power of Islam became tremendous—Jews and Christians were slaughtered, and Jerusalem fell. The pope lost control for centuries.

Let's now dig a little deeper in our investigative abyss to see if we can figure out how Lucifer, the great deceiver and accuser, who we've previously determined is also the supreme scammer, fits into the Judeo-Christian-Islamic intersecting eschatology. The Bible states Jesus was crucified and died on the Cross. "And they took Jesus, and led him away. And he bearing his cross went forth into a place called the place of a skull, which is called in the Hebrew

Golgotha: Where they crucified Him, and two other with him, on either side one, and Jesus in the midst." Multiple witnesses to crucifixion & death: a "great crowd of people."[cxliii]

In contrast, the Qur'an states he never went to the cross. "And for claiming that they killed the Messiah, Jesus, son of Mary, the messenger of GOD. In fact, they never killed him, they never crucified him - they were made to think that they did. All factions who are disputing in this matter are full of doubt concerning this issue. They possess no knowledge; they only conjecture. For certain, they never killed him."[cxliv]

Islam is looking for the return of the Prophet Jesus, born by a miracle of God without a father and the Mahdi—the Islamic Messiah. Mohammed's words give an account of the signs that will precede the coming of Jesus. We know that Christianity's prophets confirm that God is sovereign over history and is working out his purposes in accordance with an overall plan, sometimes indiscernible, but always in the hands of the Lord. However, we hope this investigation reveals what we know to be true and clears up some of the unclear.

When we again apply the traditional continuous historical context, through which Christians and Jews universally understand the Holy Bible and apply a verse-by-verse comparison, Islam comes sharply into focus as the end-time foe of God's people. In fact, the Prophet Mohammed is highly suspected by this political and theological detective as the false prophet Christianity has been keeping their eyes out for centuries. Lots of theological detectives are looking at Rome, the Vatican, and Pope Francis, but not me. This detective of deception and deceit is about to uncover another big twist in this investigation. I highly suspect Lucifer of the Bible is the Islamic god Allah.

The god Allah existed before Islam, before Muhammad, before Kadijah and her cousin Waraquah, and even before kind old uncle Abu Talib or even grandfather Abdul-Muttalib. The Arabs were polytheistic, meaning many gods. He was only one of 360 gods and was known as "the god of the crescent moon." Allah is also called "the morning/dawn star." When Mohammed came along, he declared the other 359 gods to be false and there was only Allah.

In the Bible, Lucifer is referred to as "Bel, Baal and Baassebub"[cxlv] in both the Old Testament and New Testament. They're all the same name and mean the cult of the crescent MOON GOD. The origin of Bel was Babylon. When Gideon defeated the evil Midianites upon God's command, his last act was to tear the crescent symbols off the camels' necks to show the dominance and victory of the God of Abraham, Isaac, and Jacob over Lucifer.[cxlvi]

The Bible identifies all the nations Jesus will fight when he returns, and today they are all identified Islamic nations.[cxlvii] It specifically states that he will do the same to them as Gideon did to Midian and its leaders. Just as Gideon tore down Lucifer's symbol of the crescent moon, so will Jesus tear down the crescent moon and star symbols all over the Middle East when he returns.

Islamic end times theology takes this truth and twists it: they have the Mahdi and Isa, the Muslim Jesus returning and tearing down all the CROSSES on Earth.

We know Satan's name is Lucifer, which we get from the Prophet Isaiah and the Holy Bible. "Lucifer" is the English translation of a Hebrew word that is "heylel," or "hilal."[cxlviii] He is described as Son of the Dawn or Morning. In Hebrew, the words translated are Heylel Ben Shachar. What is even more fascinating, however, is that the word Heylel, which is translated in the King James as Lucifer, is also found in Arabic, having a nearly identical meaning. Most specifically: Hilal in Arabic means Crescent Moon.

When we put the whole phrase together, Heylel Ben Shachar simply means Crescent Moon, son of the Morning Star or the Dawn—or in simpler terms, a crescent moon with a star lingering over it. Of course, this has come to be the very symbol of Allah and Islam. Yet Isaiah portrays the crescent moon and star to

195

graphically depict Lucifer himself.

Even today, nearly every Islamic country's flag carries this symbol, as does nearly every mosque brandish this symbol on the pinnacle of its dome and/or its minarets. Consider the implications of this then: the very description that the Bible uses to describe Lucifer, Islam applies to itself.

This really shouldn't surprise you. We know thus far, Lucifer wants to be God and he wants to be worshipped. For him, this is what it's all been about since he originally rebelled in Heaven, and it's his goal here in these last days. Mohammed—the first false prophet and form of Antichrist—spoke and wrote the Qur'an with the help of his very wealthy Roman Catholic wife, Kadijah, her cousin Waraquah, and even old Uncle Abu Talib.

Not surprisingly, one particular Qur'an narrative contains several of the very same elements that we find in the biblical account of the fall of Lucifer, or Satan. In the Qur'an, Surah entitled Qadr (power or fate), we find a passage that speaks directly of the dawn—when the angelic host came down from Heaven. Let's look at the Qur'an passage that describes the Night of Vision: "We have sent it to thee in the Night of Vision, what do you know of this Night of Vision. The Night of Vision is better than a thousand months. The angelic hosts descend [to earth] in it with the Spirit by command of their Lord. Peace shall it be until the rising of the Dawn Morningstar."[cxlix]

According to Islamic tradition, this event occurred on the 27th day of the month of Ramadan. It was then that Muhammad allegedly had his encounter with the "angel" who revealed the Qur'an. Ramadan is the same month during which Muslims fast from dawn to dusk, basing the fasting season on the appearance of the moon. These words, in fact, parallel Scripture regarding Lucifer, the morning star or dawn, being cast out of Heaven and taking one-third of the angels with him. The Prophet Isaiah said of Lucifer's fall, "How you have fallen from Heaven, morning star, son of the dawn. You have been cast down to the earth, you who once laid low the nations![cl] For thou hast said in thine heart, I will ascend into Heaven, I will exalt my throne above the stars of God: I will sit also up on the mount of the congregation, in the sides of the north: I will ascend above the heights of the clouds; I will be like the Most-High."[cli]

As this investigation continues, it is interesting to note that the very sin of Lucifer in this passage is defined by the phrase uttered in his heart; "I will ascend... I will be like the Most High." The word for ascend or rising in Hebrew is "Allah,"[clii]a primitive root; to ascend, intransitively (be high) or active (mount). And of course, it's the name used by Muslims for God.

In the same way that Allah has laid claim to the title of Almighty God of the Universe, despite the fact that he is simply an Arabian moon god, so also is Lucifer's desire to be exalted as an equal to God Almighty. If the divine hint found in the word

Heylel, meaning both Lucifer and Crescent Moon, is not enough, so also in the very same passage—the use of the word *Allah* for Lucifer's sin of ascending or rising to take God's place—may indeed be another prophetic hint, unveiling the identity of that ancient and very evil being hiding behind the title of Allah.

At this point of the investigation, and given the recently discovered preponderance of evidence, Lucifer's battle plan is to deceive us and do it every day. He was there in the beginning watching the fall of man to his great pleasure. He was there in Babel, played by Mr. Abaddon, the tower preconstruction project manager, and he is ever present in the troubles in the Middle East and causing so much trouble here in the United States and Europe, convincing the world his way is a better way. His desire is to bring the world together under his leadership and declare himself the Most High.

Western civilization is dying. Lucifer, the supreme scammer, has facilitated the mass migration of people in accordance with the previously mentioned United Nations Migration Compact. This document of demonic deception and deceit was signed behind the backs of the working people of the world and it has moved millions of Turkish, Middle Eastern, and mostly Muslim people into Europe over the last two decades. Europe has essentially become a home for the entire migrating Middle East. This detective of democratic death believes Europe has lost the existential will to survive. Powerful European Union member Germany, which holds tremendous self-punishing guilt due to the Holocaust, has unwittingly woven another evil web of deceit and death. This time, the web was woven in the name of peace, tolerance, unity, and humanity.

Western civilization is rainbow-blind to the stealth invasion of what will prove to be more than cultural change.

Europe has the existential malaise of a dying civilization. They are surrendering their sovereignty and legitimacy to invading armies of people who have never been afraid to tell us their evil intentions to rule the world for Islam. If Europe is now the home to anybody from the Middle East, this investigator of invasion insanity believes the United States will also fall to The Coexist Conspiracy and its open invitation of no borders, no walls, sanctuary for all. This has all been accomplished by Lucifer's foundational transformation of America's values—God, country, and family.

America, and the world at large, have failed to recognize the enemy. This detective of demonic demons believes Lucifer of the Holy Bible and Allah of the Qur'an are the same evil eschatological character. This shape-shifting demon of disguise is hiding in the synthetic stone of manmade religion and behind the fraudulent display of peace, tolerance, unity, and humanity. This supreme scammer and great deceiver are pretending to make his way, whether it's Islam or the rainbow hugs of progressive socialism; it's all anti-Christian, making it Anti-Christ. Remember what we said before; Christianity is not a religion. Beware of Intersecting Ideology.

Chapter Thirteen

The Case of the Misplaced Mother

If I were hanged on the highest hill,
Mother o' mine, O mother o' mine!
I know whose love would follow me still,
Mother o' mine, O mother o' mine!
- Rudyard Kipling -

Not a whole lot is known about Mary, the mother of Jesus.

We know she was instrumental in calling Christ's attention to a
need when Jesus performed his first miracle at the wedding in
Cana.[cliii] Mary was instrumental in calling Christ's attention to a
need and Christ responded with a miracle. Mary was present at the
crucifixion in Jerusalem, when Jesus gave her into the Apostle
John's care. She was also with the disciples in the days before the
Pentecost, and it is believed she was present at the resurrection.[cliv]

Mary's last years on Earth are not mentioned in the Holy
Bible, creating the perfect opportunity for the great deceiver and

supreme scammer to insert tradition. What is it the Bible says about tradition? "Making the word of God of none effect through your tradition, which ye have delivered: and many such like things you do."[clv] According to tradition, Mary went to Ephesus, where she experienced her "dormition."[clvi] Another tradition states that she remained in Jerusalem. Nevertheless, Pope Pius XII made the belief that Mary's body was assumed into Heaven as official Roman Catholic dogma in 1950.[clvii]

The four Roman Catholic dogmas are: Mother of God, Perpetual virginity of Mary, the Immaculate Conception, and Assumption of Mary. As a matter of evidence, the Holy Bible states Mary was the mother of Jesus and had four other sons; Joseph, James, Jude, and Simon. Because of the virgin birth, Joseph was not the father of Jesus, so these were the half-brothers of Jesus. The last three mentioned are not to be confused with those who were disciples of Jesus by the same name.[clviii]

The Scripture does not support Roman Catholic doctrine of the eternal virginity of Mary, either. They claim these others were sons of Joseph by a former wife, but there is no biblical foundation for this, nor for the perpetual virginity of Mary. The Bible only teaches us that Joseph kept her a virgin until after the birth of Jesus.[clix] The feast of the Assumption is celebrated on August 15. The Assumption was the bodily taking up of the Virgin Mary into Heaven at the end of her earthly life. According to Pope Pius XII, the Virgin Mary "having completed the course of her earthly life, was assumed body and soul into heavenly glory."[clx]

In 1854, Pope Pius IX proclaimed the dogma of the Immaculate Conception—that Mary, as the Mother of the Second Person of the Holy Trinity, was free of original sin at the moment of her conception. The feast of the Immaculate Conception is celebrated on December 8. The birthday of Mary is an old feast in the Church, celebrated on September 8 since the seventh century.

Pope Pius XII dedicated the entire human race to Mary in 1944. The Roman Catholic Church has long taught that Mary is truly the Mother of God. As a result, Roman Catholics worldwide now believe Mary, the mother of Jesus, is patroness of any good work because she is often cited as the patroness of all humanity. Mary is also associated with protecting many occupations and geographical locations.[clxi]

Roman Catholic tradition looks to Mary in the highest sense as being "immaculate"; she was free from every taint of selfishness that might obscure God's light in her being. She was then a freedom that obeyed him perfectly, and in this obedience found the fulfillment of perfect love. Tradition contends the significance of Catholic devotion to Mary is to be seen in the light of the Incarnation itself. They say the Church cannot separate the Son and the Mother and when God comes into the world through the instrumentality of one of his servants, then there is nothing surprising about the fact that his chosen instrument should have the greatest and most intimate share in the divine gift.

Roman Catholic tradition asserts Mary was empty of all egotism and she was free from all sin. Tradition tells us, God assuming Mary into Heaven was not just a glorification of a "Mother Goddess,"[clxii] it is the expression of the divine love for humanity, and a very special manifestation of God's respect for his creatures, his desire to do honor to the beings he has made in his own image, and most particularly his respect for the body which was destined to be the temple of his glory. Catholics are told all our sanctity depends on her maternal love.

Let's imagine again for a moment I am the Ghost of Signs and Wonders Past and once again, you join me as we go back in time. We are not going as far back in history as Babel; today we are traveling to Fatima, Portugal, and the year is 1917. World War I was raging and humanity was witness to some of the most hideous forms of warfare known to mankind, such as poisonous gas.

The Communist revolution was sending Russia and Eastern Europe into decades of oppressive atheistic control under authoritarian governments. In post-revolutionary Russia, the Union of Soviet Socialist Republics (USSR), also known as the Soviet Union, was formed. The Russian Empire was history, and the world had the first country to be based on Marxist socialism.[clxiii]

On May 13, 1917, an apparition of a woman reportedly dressed in white and shining brilliantly, even more than the sun, appeared to three children, saying, "Please don't be afraid of me, I'm not going to harm you."[clxiv] One of the children, named Lucia, asked her where she came from and she responded, "I come from Heaven." Lucia said the woman was holding a rosary in her hand. The woman asked the children to pray and devote themselves to the Holy Trinity and to "say the Rosary every day, to bring peace to the world and an end to the war."[clxv] When asked by one of the children who she was, the lady responded, "I am the Lady of the Rosary,"[clxvi] and she promised the children she would show the people her apparitions were true.

Following this promise by the woman, a large crowd of 700,000 people said they saw "something," saying the sun made three circles and moved around the sky in a zigzag movement which left no doubt in their minds about the truth of the apparitions seen by the children. Personally, this investigator has never witnessed or knowingly been part of mass delusion, unless of course you count President Barack Hussein Obama's repetitive promise "If you like your doctor, you can keep your doctor." I have a hard time reconciling witnesses seeing the sun moving in the sky and a report of a woman giving instructions to three children about world peace, and what criteria did the Vatican use to validate its authenticity besides the demonically inspired groupthink and signs and wonders? Nobody reported seeing the woman other than the three children who were allegedly given a message by the lady in the vision, who was concerned about the violence, war, starvation, and persecution of the Church and the pope in the twentieth century if the world did not make reparation for its sins. The lady in the vision asked for the Church to pray and offer sacrifices to God in order that peace may come upon the world, and that the trials may be averted. The lady in the vision also allegedly predicted World War II, and what Russia would do to humanity by abandoning the Christian faith and embracing Communist totalitarianism.

After the lady appeared in Fatima, Portugal, as "The Mother of God" and "The Lady of the Rosary," Roman Catholics worldwide began praying special devotions called Novenas to Fatima, which they offered throughout the world, spreading good public relations to the Muslim world. The Arabs believed the Vatican was honoring the daughter of Muhammad, whose name was Fatima, which is what the Jesuits wanted them to believe.[clxvii]

Life is Worth Living was an inspirational American television series running on television in the 1950s and '60s featuring Archbishop Fulton Sheen, who believed that the Lady of Fatima would lead to the conversion of Islam. He contended Islam was the only great post-Christian religion of the world; of course, Bishop Sheen never met AOC and The Green New Deal folks who seem to be in the process of starting one. Islam, he held, had its origin in the seventh century under Muhammad and it contained a mixture of Christianity and Judaism. Bishop Sheen felt the missionary effort of the Roman Catholic Church toward converting Islam was a failure. He though Muslims were almost unconvertible. Sheen held the Qur'an had many passages about Mary and was essentially "the bible of the Moslems." He knew the Qur'an records the accuracy of the Immaculate Conception and Virgin Birth. He also knew Muslims DO NOT accept Jesus Christ as the Son of God and in the Qur'an, Jesus is a mere prophet. He found this was the reason it was difficult for Muslims to convert to

Christianity.

We verified this earlier during our investigation and determined the good bishop was correct; the Qur'an places the history of Mary's family in a genealogy that goes back through Abraham, Noah, and Adam, clearly indicating to this investigator of innovative intrusions Lucifer has had his hoaxing hands in history since the beginning ~~scamming~~ community-organizing-the-world.

Bishop Sheen believed, as many Roman Catholics today, that Mary chose to be known as "Our Lady of Fatima" as a pledge and a sign of hope to Islam. The Roman Catholic Church's missionary strategy admittedly was and still is directed to Muslims who venerate her, hoping some will someday accept Jesus too. Sheen taught that a young Roman Catholic boy fell in love with a beautiful Muslim girl named Fatima, who converted to Catholicism. As the widely believed story goes, the young husband was so in love with Fatima he had the name of the town where they lived in Portugal changed. This investigation thus far concludes the very place where the apparition of the shining woman dressed in white, who is now known as "Our Lady," appeared in 1917 and she holds an undeniable historical connection to Fatima, the daughter of Mohammed.

Years after World War II, Pope Pius XII told the world about his dancing sun vision, which brought Fatima back in the news again and more importantly, into Catholic awareness. Pope Pius was the only one to see this vision. As a result, a group of followers has grown into a Blue Army worldwide, totaling millions of faithful Roman Catholics who are now ready to die for the blessed virgin.[clxviii] Bishop Sheen said, "Our Lady's appearances at Fatima marked the turning point in the history of the world's 350 million Muslims. After the death of his daughter Fatima, Muhammad wrote that she is the most holy of all women in Paradise, next to Mary." As we said earlier, Bishop Sheen taught that Mary chose to be known as "Our Lady of Fatima"[clxix] as a sign and a pledge that the Muslims who believe in Christ's virgin birth will come to believe in his divinity. Bishop Sheen pointed out the pilgrim virgin statues of Our Lady of Fatima were enthusiastically received by Muslims in Africa, India, and elsewhere, and that many Muslims are now coming to a knowledge of Jesus through Mary. Is this movement of The Coexist Conspiracy going anywhere? Could we see a Cathlo-Islamic Religion with a new and improved Lady of Fatima in the form of Marian-Muslim somewhere in the making? Don't think for a minute it's not possible. Remember back in chapter six, we investigated the confusion caper and finding out much to our surprise the Statue of Liberty is actually a Muslim refugee.[clxx] What would that look like? We already established Islam has adopted many Judeo-Christian elements into its own religion.

Chrislam is a new religious movement in the United States, having roots in Nigeria. It appears to promote unity and humanity to resolve war between Christianity and Islam. This detective of deceitful dualism detects, while it is undeniable that there are many similarities between Christianity, Judaism, and Islam—Chrislam is a pure hoax because Islam and Christianity are diametrically opposed on the most important item: the identity of Jesus Christ. True Christianity declares Jesus to be God incarnate. The deity of Christ is non-negotiable for Christians because without his deity, Jesus's death on the cross would not have been sufficient to be the atoning sacrifice for the sins of the entire world. He had to be God incarnate.

In contrast, Islam adamantly rejects the deity of Christ. The Qur'an declares the idea that Jesus is God to be blasphemy.[clxxi] Belief in the deity of Jesus Christ is considered *shirk* ("polytheism") to Muslims. Further, Islam flatly denies the death of Christ on the cross.[clxxii]

The most crucial doctrine of the Christian faith is rejected in Islam. As a result, the two religions are absolutely not compatible. With all the bizarre demonic occurrences in the world today, it would take some Marian-Muslim-Chrislam-Lady shining like the morning dawn over New York similar to "Our Lady of Liberty Enlightening the World" to get me to notice. Maybe if the government-controlled media reported Lady Liberty walked on the water across of New York Harbor and sat down in Yankee Stadium watching them lose once again to the Red Sox, I might be interested enough to check it out. For the most part, religion is a racket, and we are being scammed into a one-world order—one way or another. In the meantime, beware the Misplaced Mother.

Chapter Fourteen
The Case of the Woven Web

Little Miss Muffet sat on her tuffet, eating her curds eating and whey.
Along came a spider who sat down beside her
And frightened Miss Muffet away.

Little Miss Muffet was an insightful young lady. She must

have recalled Mary Howlett's poem about the *Spider and the Fly*. The

poem opens with a dialogue between a predatory scammer, played

by the spider, and the Unexceptional American, played by the fly.

The spider attempts to draw the fly into the parlor of his total

control. The spider then entices the fly by saying his parlor has no

borders, no walls, and sanctuary for all. Mother Goose's Muffet

was known to be a witty and wise little girl and wasn't entertaining

the fly's compliments and doublespeak, and recognized the risk of

getting dragged into the spider's parlor never to return from the new one-world order. She recognized the web of deceit in plenty of time and ran for her life. The poem didn't say any of that, but you get my point.

Continuing to follow our classical historical investigative approach into *The Coexist Conspiracy*, we now need to reach back into the short history of our own case studies to summarize our findings.

In the case study of the Delusional Dreamer, we concluded the deceit and deception woven through the globalist mind is the delusional belief: No borders, no walls, and sanctuary for all, are essential to eliminate war and any potential for conflict. We concluded "Imagine" is now the well-established anthem of the progressive liberal left in America. We also considered the world and its scammers had been whispering sweet words of tempting coexistence in John's ears for many years.

In the case of the Conniving Con, the investigation revealed the quest to coexist has been championed by globalist elites since the end of World War II. We learned it's a racket to harness people and their wealth on a global scale, with or without their complicit knowledge, by examining several corporate and individual scammers. We also learned how these doers of dastardly deeds adjust the scams frequently to stay ahead of law enforcement. Most importantly, we uncovered how and why many influential political figures are working this supreme global scam. We highlighted their role and function, offering the titles supreme scammer, the super scammer, and soldier scammers. We established that one-world-government con artists have been manipulating the political and financial events of the world with their global organizing efforts for decades. We examined several different cons, scams, and double deals in an effort to get a full understanding of how the web of deceit is woven through *The Coexist Conspiracy*.

In the case study of the Synthetic Stone, we reviewed the first failed attempt by mankind to community-organize the world into a one-world order. We witnessed the woven web of deceit as we were transported back to the last preconstruction meeting for the city of Babel. We saw firsthand the bait and switch scam to replace the original plans to build with natural stone and use synthetic stone in the form of manmade brick. We investigated Big Pharma and found that replacement of natural with synthetic has been a web of deception woven through every industry from the construction sites of the building trades to the hospital and nursing home floors of our medical industry. It has been a major stumbling block in mankind's self-proclaimed drive towards unity and humanity without seeing what beauty exists in the natural stone and *The Great Rock* [clxxiii] provided by our Creator. We concluded humanity wasn't meant to die from heart disease, stroke, diabetes, or from cancer. Manmade bricks, manmade medications like synthetic antibiotics and opioids, processed synthetic inside aisles of the grocery store foods are a delusional dream, a conniving con, and part and parcel of *The Coexist Conspiracy*.

In the case of the Organizing Scheme, we studied Saul and his not a rock and roll band of Alinskyites and community organizers who were taking it to the streets, equipping young America with future generations of radical socialists, anarchists, and wannabe communists. We learned Hillary Clinton knew Super Scammer Saul well, and President Barack Hussein Obama and a number of other highly influential government officials are now the soldier scammers for the global elite in the conspiratorial effort to community-organize the world, harnessing its people and their wealth for the supreme scammer to call his own.

The case of the Fraudulent Financier reviewed publicly available newspapers, magazines, books, and Internet to reveal that one of the richest men in the world today is George Soros. We suspected, but found out he is in fact NOT the supreme scammer.

He is, however, a highly skilled financial facilitator and super scammer, and has woven his web of deceit by spreading his wealth through every liberal progressive socialist organization, supporting the now and coming one-world order. Uncle George is not just a soldier scammer like Saul, Bill, Hill, and Barry O in the community-organizing effort; he's a mere prince doing his king's bidding. His king is the supreme scammer and great deceiver.

The case of the Confusion Caper concluded that a collaboration of conniving cons controls the United Nations. Conspiratorial controlled confusion is the description of something that looks out of control yet is functioning according to the designed scam. The scammer is a wordsmith, and has made clear to the co-investigative reader during the study that if you're confused and trying to determine what's real and what's fake, the scammers have you right where they want you. The supreme scammer is the author of confusion and deceit, and it is he whose isin and rebellion are shaking this world like never before. He is responsible for weaving his plan through the organizations and institutions of the world in an effort to control people by keeping them connived, confused, and looking to government for answers. We also got the first big reveal of the investigation. We uncovered and provided documented evidence the Statue of Liberty is Muslim refugee.[clxxiv] The Supreme Scammer's woven web of deceit and deception is invasive, infective, and is using the United Nations as a conduit for establishing a one-world order.

In the case of the Social Justice Warrior, we learned the definition of social justice varies with the organization or individual social justice warrior defining it for you. Their common themes include human rights and economic equal distribution of wealth and resources. This social justice term has been redefined by secular liberal and so-called progressive thinkers; however, this writer holds a very different view of what it means. A social justice warrior or soldier scammer, by this writer's definition, is a street-wise scammer advocating a socially constructed, uniform, government-controlled distribution of society's advantages and disadvantages. We looked at organizations such as Rainbow-Push, Antifa, Black Lives Matter, and others caught in the woven web of deceit of the supreme scammer, who is a great deceiver.

The case of the Unexceptional American rattled this investigator of political and theological truth. Like a real detective walking in on a bloody crime scene, I had to cover my nose and mouth in an effort to not smell the sulfur stink of the great accuser, who is a great deceiver and supreme scammer, while investigating this dude. We concluded that the Unexceptional American is all about legal abortion, infanticide, same-sex marriage, and local library-sponsored drag queen story time in the children's room is now leading the world, shaking his unity and humanity rainbow-colored fists at his Creator.

In the case of the Religion Racket, the second big reveal of this interwoven investigation is the supreme scammer has used world religion to lead mankind away from the truth, and we deferred to scammer Saul Alinsky, who correctly identified the first community organizer as Lucifer of the Bible. We learned Lucifer has been skillfully duping people down through the ages by convincing them of their need to reach up to their Creator through tradition, rites, rituals, and good works instead of recognizing the Creator himself already reached down to mankind 2,000 years ago through his Son, Jesus Christ, and his redemptive work is *finished*.

In the case of the Intersecting Ideology, we learned Lucifer the supreme scammer has facilitated the mass migration of people in accordance with the dictates of the United Nations Migration Compact. We also learned this document of demonic deception and deceit was signed behind the backs of the working people of the world, and it has moved millions of Turkish, Middle Eastern, and mostly Muslim people into Europe over the last two decades. We found the United States and world at large have failed to recognize the enemy. This detective of demonic demons has uncovered the third big reveal—Lucifer of the Holy Bible and

Allah of the Qur'an are the same evil eschatological character. He is charged with being the shape-shifting demon of disguise who has been hiding in the synthetic stone of manmade religion and behind the fraudulent display of peace, tolerance, unity, and humanity.

In the case of the Misplaced Mother, we found a historical connection between the Vatican and Islam. We learned of an emerging world religion called Chrislam and speculated, with all the bizarre demonic occurrences in the world today, old Lucifer/Allah might utilize some fancy Marian-Muslim-Chrislam-Refugee-Lady shining like the morning dawn over New York similar to "Our Lady of Liberty Enlightening the World" at some point to get the world's attention. You can tell she already got my attention and she hasn't even run across New York Harbor. Yet.

Conclusion
The Case of the Conquering King

*"Calvary's summit shall I trace,
View the heights and depths of grace,
Count the purple drops and say,
Thus, my sins were washed away."*[clxxv]
Charles Haddon Spurgeon

I hope by the end of this political and theological investigation, my dear sidekick, you will believe as I do; the way out of all this horror to come is when Jesus Christ snatches his followers out of this rapid descent into a period of great trouble for the world the Bible calls the Great Tribulation. The way this detective of doctrinal deception figures unbelievers will have seven years under the new one-world *disorder* before the end of the world, as we know it, comes.

Jesus described this judgment to come as a time of trouble the world has never seen or will ever see again.[clxxvi]

In the Bible, the ultimate evidence proving the crimes against humanity perpetrated by the supreme scammer Lucifer in the past, also reveals a detailed account of the horrors, destruction, and desolation he will soon inflict upon this planet. The Supreme Scammer has taken thousands of years convincing us we can socially construct and community organize a better world than the Creator of all.

The supreme scam, we have determined, is being thrust on the world's inhabitants by the global elites in an effort to convince us to eliminate war, violence, hatred, racism, sexism, homophobia, Islamophobia, and have a fair distribution of the world's wealth and resources; we must pursue a new, improved, supersized one-world order to glorify our unity and humanity without seeking divine intervention. The rub in this ruse is Lucifer, the supreme scammer, includes his community-organizing to unlock the abyss in the Earth's core, letting hordes of demonic creatures out to roam the Earth with power to inflict torment like scorpions. It will be such a time of terrible torment and horror that people will want to kill themselves to escape it, but according to the Bible, they won't be able to die. They will be in a living hell.[clxxvii]

Why will there be such awful judgment upon the Earth? Don't miss the forest for the trees! Because the world has been forsaking the laws of God. Sin against God has its own inevitable consequence—death. However, God has given us the way to a meaningful and prosperous life through his one and only Son, Jesus Christ.

The Bible tells us that the people still left on Earth in the last days "repented not of the works of their hands, that they should not worship devils, and idols neither repenting of their murders, sorceries and fornication nor their thefts."[clxxviii]

Today, many people are seeking the counsel of Lucifer when they are looking for guidance. They seek the advice of horoscopes, fortune-tellers, Ouija boards, psychics, mediums, secular psychiatrists, and worst of all...the world's manmade religions! People are going through their surface-living lives worshiping idols and the "god of this world"[clxxix]—Lucifer.

Evidence reveals everyone is bowing to some manmade object of worship—some goal, ambition, political principle, or even some entertainment god. These folks are on their way to eternal life without knowing the peace, joy, and love of our King, Jesus Christ. People will always find something to worship besides Almighty God if they do not know Jesus Christ. The world today is ridiculing, laughing at, and mocking Christians for believing in Jesus Christ.

With all these worldly idols, scams, schemes, and sin in our lives...why don't we get what we deserve? People often say things like...that murderer *deserves* to get the electric chair...when they hear in the news about a horrible crime. I've been heard to say myself, "I think I'll have that piece of cake. I worked hard today, I *deserve* it." I hear the word *deserve* being used all the time.

It's human nature to expect people would get what they deserve. It's a matter of fact society looks for justice to be applied in this world. When we hear about terrible crimes of abuse against children and the scams, schemes, and rackets targeting the elderly, we're outraged. When a homeless veteran is beaten to death for the pure sport of it by lost souls wandering the streets, some people call for the death penalty. For the most part, when I or anybody else compares their sin to that of a murderer, thief, or child abuser, we think we look pretty good on the scale we have made up for ourselves. The scale I once used looks something like this: Jesus Christ, who equals sinless perfection, is on the top of my scale. The apostles are somewhere close by, but not at the top. Adolph Hitler and people like him are on the bottom, and I fall somewhere in between. Obviously, I thought of myself on my personal scale as being farther away from Hitler and a little closer to the apostles. Not too bad, I guess. However, if I really want to be honest with myself and look at all the things that I have done wrong and do wrong, I can see that I easily "fall short of the glory of God."[clxxx]

If I made a list of every little scamming, scheming thought and actual wrong that I have done in my life, the reality is that I wouldn't be as close on my scale to apostles as I had previously thought. The Bible tells us, "the wages of sin is death."[clxxxi] The Good News is that Jesus finished the work of redemption and he made himself a substitution for you and me. Christ took the punishment that mankind deserves.

When I truly reflect upon what Jesus did for us schemers and scammers on that cross, I am moved to tears in a major emotional meltdown of sorrow, love, and joy. Our wonderful Savior was stripped down and tied to a post to be whipped. A crown of thorns was thrust onto his head. He was beaten, mocked, and forced to carry the cross to Calvary. There he was laid on the cross and nails were hammered into his bone and flesh. He was then left to die hanging on that heavy timber for six hours. In addition to the physical pain of this torturous death, our Lord was rejected by the world and his friends turned their backs on him.

Yet, this was a victory over sin itself…yours, mine, and everybody else's who accepts his message. The prophet Isaiah says, "He bore the sins of many,"[clxxxii] and Christ had come to this sinful world to set an example of supreme self-sacrifice and love. The Bible also says "He is the atoning sacrifice for our sins, and not only for ours, but also for the sins of the world."[clxxxiii]

Are you still asking yourself if Jesus forgives all your scams, schemes, and sin? The answer is…YES! God's forgiveness includes our past, present, and future sins. The fact is that we are justified and pardoned, and we can never be unpardoned. Christians can never more be condemned. Those who do not believe this are sadly missing the point. God will not pardon a person and then punish him later. What would have been the point of Christ's work here on Earth if that were the case? Jesus said with his last dying breath and giving up his spirit, "It is finished."[clxxxiv] Jesus was telling the world that the entire work of redemption had been brought to completion. The Greek translation for "It is finished" is "Paid in full." One cannot pay more for a debt that has already been paid if it was paid in full.

> *"Here's a pardon for transgressions past;*
> *It matters not how black their cast:*
> *And, O my soul with wonder view,*
> *for sins to come there's pardon too"* [clxxxv]
> Charles Haddon Spurgeon

While unloading on the fish pier, one of my coworkers asked me, "Can your Jesus forgive me of all my sin?" He told me he had some difficult times during his early years that had greatly impacted where he was now at midlife. Substance abuse and a string of failed relationships had life-long effects. These difficulties, he stated, while now in the past, had separated him from every good thing in life. He was clearly in spiritual pain and searching for God.

Our conversation turned to the power of sin and how it is addictive and controlling. I told him sin is like a drug, and it can take over and interrupt our lives and God's plan and purpose for us. When we finished working for the day, I showed him in my Bible where Jesus said, "Everyone who sins is a slave to sin."[clxxxvi] I shared with him that sin has had its hold on me, too; however, I was confident that through my faith and belief in Jesus Christ, I knew I was completely forgiven dept paid in full! God's promise is, "I will forgive their wickedness and will never again remember their sins."[clxxxvii] Jesus took all my sin with him to the cross. "It is finished."[clxxxviii]

"Amazing Grace How Sweet the Sound that Saved a Wretch like me!
I once was lost, but now am found was blind but now I see."
- John Henry Newton –

John Henry Newton (July 24, 1725–December 21, 1807) wrote the hymn "Amazing Grace." He was an Englishman, an Anglican clergyman and former slave-ship captain. Grace is often described as "undeserved acceptance and love received from another." In the sense of divine grace towards mankind, it refers to the undeserved favor of God by providing us salvation instead of condemnation and death. History reports that John Newton knew God's grace firsthand. As a slave-ship captain, John Newton was involved in what has proven throughout history to be one of the world's most horrible sins, the slavery of others. When John Newton accepted Christ, his whole life turned around and he fought against slavery for the rest of his life.

"But suppose a man can be so changed that just as freely as he was accustomed
to curse he now delights to pray,
and just as heartily as he hated religion he now finds pleasure in it,
and just earnestly as he sinned he now delights to be obedient to the Lord.
This is a wonder, a miracle which man cannot accomplish,
marvel which only the grace of God can work and which gives God His highest
glory." clxxxix
-Charles Haddon Spurgeon-

The saving grace of Jesus Christ is the most powerful thing in all of God's creation. My grandmother told me many years ago that religion is something made up by men and that grace is a gift of God. Grace is a major biblical doctrine that sets Christianity apart from other religions. No other belief system, religion, or god asserts that divine grace is its scriptural tenet.

The Bible says, "Grace and truth came through Jesus Christ."[cxc]Jesus said, "I am the way and the truth and the life. No one comes to the Father except through me."[cxci]There is no other way. John Henry Newton knew this and by God's divine grace, experienced his conversion to Christ and the forgiveness of his sin.

Whenever I bring up the subject of God's grace to someone, I am asked the same question. "Doesn't this give people the license to scam, scheme, and sin?" and the answer is absolutely not! The Holy Spirit and the assurance of God's grace will help us through our temptation. Never let us forget that when we struggle with sin, we are in good company. The Apostle Paul struggled with his own sin, saying, "What a wretched man I am! Who will rescue me from this body of death? Thanks, be to God through Jesus Christ our Lord!"[cxcii]

Before I close, I need to ask you one more question. Are you still asking yourself, "If this is true, how will I escape this impending destruction and horror to come?" Here it is, four simple steps.

1. **Recognize you're a sinner.** The Bible says, *"As it is written, there is none righteous, no, not one,"*[xciii] and *"For all have sinned, and come short of the glory of God."*[xciv]

2. **Recognize that Jesus died for you.** The apostle Peter tells us, *"For Christ also hath once suffered for sins, the just for the unjust, that he might bring us to God, being put to death in the flesh, but quickened by the Spirit."*[xcv]

3. **Repent of your sins.** The Book of Acts, *"Repent ye therefore, and be converted, that your sins may be blotted out, when the times of refreshing shall come from the presence of the Lord."*[xcvi]

4. **Receive Jesus as your Savior.** The Bible assures us, *"For God so loved the world, that he gave his only begotten Son, that whosoever believeth in him should not perish, but have everlasting life,"* [xcvii] and, *"Come unto me, all ye that labor and are heavy laden, and I will give you rest."* [xcviii]

"Let the words of my mouth, and the meditation of my heart, be acceptable in thy sight, O LORD, my strength, and my redeemer." [xcix]

Shalom
Brother Gabe

Truth

END NOTES

[i] https://www.biography.com/news/john-lennon-imagine-song-facts

[ii] https://www.mercurynews.com/2017/04/30/can-we-all-just-get-along-rodney-kings-question-still-matters/

[iii] https://www.olympic.org/news/pyeongchang-2018-welcomes-the-world-with-a-message-of-peace-and-hope

[iv] https://www.biography.com/people/victor-lustig-20657385

[vi] Ibid

[vii] Holy Bible Genesis 11

[viii] https://nypost.com/2010/12/11/bernie-madoffs-son-mark-commits-suicide/

[ix] https://www.nytimes.com/2018/05/25/opinion/sunday/meat-antibiotics-organic-farming.html

[x] https://amazingbeautifulworld.net/interesting-facts/know-egyptians-applied-moldy-bread-infected

[xi] https://www.acs.org/content/acs/en/education/whatischemistry/landmarks/flemingpenicillin.html

[xii] https://www.cdc.gov/vitalsigns/opioids/index.html

[xiii] https://www.medpagetoday.com/publichealthpolicy/publichealth/57336

[xiv] HTTPS://WWW.CDC.GOV/VITALSIGNS/OPIOIDS/INDEX.HTML

[xv] https://www.nbcnews.com/news/us-news/fentanyl-deaths-mexican-oxy-pills-hit-arizona-hard-n971536

[xvi] https://www.britannica.com/biography/Saul-Alinsky

[xvii] http://www.areachicago.org/the-woodlawn-organization/

[xviii] https://www.britannica.com/biography/Saul-Alinsky

[xix] http://www1.cbn.com/cbnnews/us/2017/july/drag-queen-storytime-for-kids-at-boston-public-library-is-not-fiction

[xx] https://www.theguardian.com/world/2008/apr/14/barackobama.uselections2008

[xxi] https://www.washingtontimes.com/news/2012/sep/10/barry-was-muslim/

[xxii] https://www.investors.com/politics/editorials/media-ignores-obama-alinsky-rules-for-radicals/

[xxiii] Ibid
https://www.americanthinker.com/articles/2018/05/barack_obamas_world_as_it_should_be.html

[xxiv] http://www.freerepublic.com/focus/f-news/3451533/posts

[xxv] Rules for Radicals

[xxvi] https://www.youtube.com/watch?v=XKGdkqfBICw

[xxvii] https://www.britannica.com/biography/Saul-Alinsky

[xxviii] https://townhall.com/tipsheet/kevinglass/2012/09/17/flashback-obama-calls-americans-bitter-clingers-n718551

[xxix] http://www.cnn.com/2009/US/07/22/harvard.gates.interview/

[xxx] https://www.mrc.org/special-reports/special-report-george-soros-godfather-left

[xxxi] https://www.youtube.com/watch?v=W8Id0-Lsyr0

[xxxii] https://www.nytimes.com/2002/12/21/business/soros-is-found-guilty-in-france-on-

charges-of-insider-trading.html
xxxiii https://www.mrc.org/commentary/soros-spends-over-48-million-funding-media-organizations
xxxiv Ibid.
xxxv https://www.opensocietyfoundations.org/explainers/open-society-foundations-and-george-soros
xxxvi Ibid
xxxvii https://newrepublic.com/article/74330/the-speculator
xxxviii Ibid.
xxxix https://newrepublic.com/article/74330/the-speculator
xl Orwell, George, 1984
xli https://www.gishgallop.com/sesame-street-announces-new-transgender-character/
xlii https://www.pbs.org/newshour/extra/tag/transgender-in-america/
xliii Rules for Radicals
xliv https://refugeesmigrants.un.org/migration-compact
xlv https://www.refugeesinternational.org/global-compacts?gclid=CjwKCAiA8OjjBRB4EiwAMZe6y6IgiwfM50eLQZ5_IX2-gLypgaOy_hLdFKldYhCNOp86OF5blHmPjhoCspkQAvD_BwE
xlvi https://www.georgesoros.com/2016/09/20/why-im-investing-500-million-in-migrants/
xlvii https://www.georgesoros.com/2016/09/20/why-im-investing-500-million-in-migrants/
xlviii https://obamawhitehouse.archives.gov/the-press-office/2016/06/30/fact-sheet-white-house-launches-call-action-private-sector-engagement-
xlix Orwell, George 1984
l https://www.simplypsychology.org/cognitive-dissonance.html
li http://www.un.org/en/universal-declaration-human-rights/
lii https://refugeesmigrants.un.org/migration-compact
liii https://www.smithsonianmag.com/smart-news/statue-liberty-was-originally-muslim-woman-180957377/
liv https://www.amazon.com/Common-Good-Robert-B-Reich/dp/052552049X
lv https://www.history.com/topics/black-history/plessy-v-ferguson
lvi https://rainbowpush.org/
lvii https://blacklivesmatter.com/about/
lviii https://blacklivesmatter.com/about/
lix https://insider.foxnews.com/2017/06/06/black-lives-matter-black-only-memorial-day-picnic-tucker-carlson-lisa-durden
lx Ibid.
lxi D'Souza, Dinesh *The Big Lie* Pages 18-19, Regenary Books 2017
lxii Lukianoff, Greg *Freedom From Speech*
lxiii https://www.merriam-webster.com/dictionary/hate%20speech
lxiv https://www.huffingtonpost.com/entry/opinion-miller-schlossberg-harassment_us_5b018833e4b07309e0598e4e
lxv https://www.washingtonpost.com/news/volokh-conspiracy/wp/2017/06/19/supreme-court-unanimously-reaffirms-there-is-no-hate-speech-exception-to-the-first-amendment/?utm_term=.905b1f12a8a6

lxvi https://www.washingtonexaminer.com/opinion/chelsea-clinton-thanks-abortion-for-being-good-for-the-economy

lxvii https://www.lifesitenews.com/news/one-world-trade-center-lit-up-to-celebrate-abortion-includes-a-memorial-to

lxviii https://www.breitbart.com/entertainment/2017/09/06/martha-plimpton-best-abortion-seattle/

lxix https://www.thedailybeast.com/michelle-wolf-unloads-on-anti-abortion-activists-god-bless-abortions

lxx http://www.gty.org/resources/Sermons/80-425/We-Will-Not-Bow

lxxi https://www.fcdflegal.org/david-daleiden-asks-supreme-court-to-stop-planned-parenthoods-suppression-of-his-first-amendment-rights/

lxxii http://video.foxnews.com/v/4464998729001/fox-news-reporting-planned-parenthood-the-hidden-harvest/?intcmp=hpvid1#sp=show-clips

lxxiii http://www.nyu.edu/projects/sanger/aboutms/index.php

lxxiv https://www.liveaction.org/news/politifact-says-true-planned-parenthood-americas-largest-abortion-provider/

lxxv https://www.breitbart.com/politics/2015/10/13/thank-god-abortion-providers-episcopal-methodist-clergy-bless-abortion-clinic/

lxxvi http://www.breitbart.com/big-government/2015/10/13/thank-god-abortion-providers-episcopal-methodist-clergy-bless-abortion-clinic/

lxxvii https://www.thenewamerican.com/world-news/north-america/item/29320-christian-canadian-law-school-denied-accreditation-because-of-its-belief-in-traditional-marriage

lxxviii https://www.bizjournals.com/atlanta/news/2017/12/20/court-upholds-firing-of-former-atlanta-fire-chief.html

lxxix https://www.nbcnews.com/feature/nbc-out/kentucky-clerk-jailed-over-gay-marriage-licenses-loses-re-election-n933451

lxxx Holy Bible 1 Corinthian 13:6

lxxxi https://www.apa.org/pi/lgbt/resources/history.html

lxxxii http://quotesyes.com/2013/10/10/george-carlin-got-arrested-with-lenny-bruce/

lxxxiii https://www.ecowatch.com/asbestos-industry-knew-and-kept-secret-for-decades-that-their-product--1891149266.html

lxxxiv 1990s. https://www.ecowatch.com/asbestos-industry-knew-and-kept-secret-for-decades-that-their-product-1891149266.html

lxxxv https://www.heartland.org/news-opinion/news/asbestos-removal-our-most-costly-environmental-scam?source=policybot

lxxxvi http://www.nelsonearthday.net/nelson/

lxxxvii https://www.npr.org/2019/02/07/691997301/rep-alexandria-ocasio-cortez-releases-green-new-deal-outline

peace-founder-global-warming-hoax-pushed-corrupt-scientists-hooked-government-grants/

lxxxix https://www.bostonherald.com/2014/04/25/carr-a-numbingly-stupid-idea-from-mr-frosty/

xc Ibid

xci United Nations Conference on Environment & Development Rio de Janerio, Brazil, 3 to

14 June 1992

xcii https://www.goodreads.com/quotes/251836-we-re-so-self-important-everybody-s-going-to-save-something-now-save

xciii https://www.goodreads.com/quotes/251836-we-re-so-self-important-everybody-s-going-to-save-something-now-save

xciv https://www.washingtonpost.com/archive/lifestyle/1980/01/27/the-education-of-shirley-mount-hufstedler/53577ec5-9548-4ac4-86d5-ffa9f0bd60b6/?utm_term=.d8b1cfe255a5

xcv ibid

xcvi https://www.britannica.com/biography/Nikita-Sergeyevich-Khrushchev

xcvii https://www.merriam-webster.com/dictionary/nationalism xcvii

xcviii https://www.merriam-webster.com/dictionary/white%20supremacist

xcix https://www.merriam-webster.com/dictionary/white%20nationalist

c https://encyclopedia.ushmm.org/content/en/article/documenting-numbers-of-victims-of-the-holocaust-and-nazi-persecution

ci Hitler, Chapter 11 *Mein Kampf*

cii https://www.breitbart.com/immigration/2019/04/01/pope-francis-disses-trumps-wall-compares-populists-to-hitler/

ciii Ibid

civ https://www.dictionary.com/browse/religion

cv Holy Bible John 19:30

cvi https://www.theguardian.com/commentisfree/belief/2009/jun/26/religion-philosophy

cvii https://www.theguardian.com/commentisfree/belief/2009/jun/26/religion-philosophy

cviii https://www.theguardian.com/commentisfree/belief/2009/jun/26/religion-philosophy

cix Ibid

cx Holy Bible Ephesians 2:2

cxi Ibid

cxii Holy Bible Colossians 1:3

cxiii Holy Bible 2 Timothy 2:26

cxiv Holy Bible 1 John 5:19

cxv Holy Bible Ephesians 2:2

cxvi Holy Bible Ephesians 2:8-9

cxvii http://www.gallup.com/poll/27877/americans-more-likely-believe-god-than-devil-Heaven-more-than-hell.aspx

cxviii Holy Bible

cxix Holy Bible (Matthew 4:8 NIV).

cxx Holy Bible (Matthew 4:10 NIV

cxxi Holy Bible Genesis

cxxii Holy Bible Matthew 24:2.

cxxiii http://www.thedailybeast.com/articles/2014/12/07/does-pope-francis-believe-christians-and-muslimsworship-the-same-god.html

cxxiv https://www.vocabulary.com/dictionary/eschatology

cxxv https://www.myjewishlearning.com/article/who-is-the-messiah/

cxxvi https://www.britannica.com/topic/mahdi

cxxvii https://www.worldatlas.com/articles/christian-denominations-by-the-numbers.html

cxxviii https://www.bibleplaces.com/westernwall/

cxxix http://www.oxfordislamicstudies.com/article/opr/t125/e5

cxxx

cxxxi https://www.islamiclandmarks.com/syria/monastery-of-bahira-the-monk

cxxxii Holy Bible Zachariah 12:2

cxxxiii https://www.jpost.com/Not-Just-News/Jerusalem-Day-City-of-peace-403116

cxxxiv https://www.history.com/topics/ancient-history/ancient-rome

cxxxv https://www.oikoumene.org/en/press-centre/news/pope-francis-says-pilgrimage-to-uae-is-a-new-page-in-christian-islam-dialogue

cxxxvi Ibid.

cxxxvii Ibid

cxxxviii Rules for Radicals

cxxxix https://www.britannica.com/biography/Khadijah

cxl http://www.oxfordislamicstudies.com/article/opr/t125/e2487

cxli http://aboutislam.net/counseling/ask-about-islam/prophet-break-idols-kaabah/

cxlii http://civictribune.com/pope-francis-at-white-house-koran-and-holy-bible-are-the-same/

cxliii Holy Bible John 19:16-18:

cxliv Qur'an Surah 4:157-159

cxlv Holy Bible Isaiah 46:1, Jeremiah 50:2, 51:44

cxlvi Holy Bible Judges 8:21

cxlvii Holy Bible Psalm 83

cxlviii Strong's Hebrew Concordance, H1966

cxlix Qur'an Surah 97:1-5

cl Holy Bible Matt. 12:46; 13:55; Mark 6:3; John 2:12; 7:3, 5, 10; Acts 1:14; 1 Cor. 9:5; Gal. 1:19

cli Holy Bible Isaiah 14:12-14

clii Strong's Hebrew Greek Dictionary H5927

cliii http://catholicstraightanswers.com/what-do-we-mean-by-the-sleep-of-mary-or-the-dormition-of-mary/

cliv https://www.catholic.org/saints/saint.php?saint_id=4967

clv Holy Bible Mark 7:13

clvi http://catholicstraightanswers.com/what-do-we-mean-by-the-sleep-of-mary-or-the-dormition-of-mary/

clvii https://www.ewtn.com/faith/teachings/marye6.htm

clviii Matt. 12:46; 13:55; Mark 6:3; John 2:12; 7:3, 5, 10; Acts 1:14; 1 Cor. 9:5; Gal. 1:19.

clix Holy Bible Matthew. 1:18-25

clx

clxi https://www.catholic.org/saints/saint.php?saint_id=4967

clxii Ibid.

clxiii https://www.history.com/this-day-in-history/ussr-established
clxiv https://www.catholicnewsagency.com/news/everything-you-need-to-know-about-fatima-part-1-15388
clxv https://www.the-american-catholic.com/2010/02/03/bishop-sheen-on-fatima/
clxvi catholicstraightanswers.com/what-do-we-mean-by-the-sleep-of-mary-or-the-dormition-of-mary/

clxvii https://www.the-american-catholic.com/2010/02/03/bishop-sheen-on-fatima/

clxviii https://www.bluearmy.com
clxix https://www.the-american-catholic.com/2010/02/03/bishop-sheen-on-fatima/
clxx https://www.smithsonianmag.com/smart-news/statue-liberty-was-originally-muslim-woman-180957377/
clxxi Qur'an Surah 5:17.
clxxii Qur'an 4:157–158
clxxiii https://www.greatrockchurch.org/know-jesus
clxxiv https://www.smithsonianmag.com/smart-news/statue-liberty-was-originally-muslim-woman-180957377/
clxxv Spurgeon, Charles Haddon. *Spurgeon's Sermons Volume 3-4*. New York, New York: Robert Carter & Brothers, 1883.

clxxvi Holy Bible Matthew Chapter 24
clxxvii Ibid.
clxxviii Ibid.
clxxix 2 Corinthians 4:4
clxxx Holy Bible Romans 3:23
clxxxi Holy Bible Romans 6:23
clxxxii Holy Bible Isaiah 53:12
clxxxiii Holy Bible1 John 2:2
clxxxiv Holy Bible John 19:30
clxxxv Ibid.
clxxxvi Hole Bible John 8:34
clxxxvii Holy Bible Jeremiah 31:34; Hebrews 8:12
clxxxviii Holy Bible John 19:30
clxxxix Ibid.
cxc Holy Bible John 1:17
cxci Holy Bible John 14: 6 NIV
cxcii Holy Bible Romans 7:24-25
cxciii Holy Bible Romans 3:10
cxciv Holy Bible Romans 3:23
cxcv Holy Bible 1 Peter 3:18
cxcvi Holy Bible Acts 3:19
cxcvii Holy Bible John 3:16
cxcviii Holy Bible John 3:10
cxcix Holy Bible Psalm 19:14

Made in the USA
Middletown, DE
25 June 2020